D0193103

45 GREAT
GIFTS TO MAKE

Jean Greenhowe

45 GREAT GIFTS TO MAKE

Jean Greenhowe

A DAVID & CHARLES CRAFT BOOK

To my daughter Victoria, with special thanks for typing the manuscript

ACKNOWLEDGEMENTS

The designs in this book were originally featured in *Woman's Weekly* magazine and I would like to express my thanks to the Editor and all Home Department staff for their assistance and co-operation during the preparation of all the material included.

The author and publishers also wish to thank IPC magazines, publishers of *Woman's Weekly*, for their kind permission to reproduce their photographs.

I am also indebted to Vera Wray of The Craft Centre, Aberdeen, for her helpful advice on many craft materials.

First published as *Jean Greenhowe's Bazaar Bestsellers* 1987

Text and patterns © Jean Greenhowe 1987, 1988
Photographs © IPC Magazines 1987, 1988

British Library Cataloguing in Publication Data
Greenhowe, Jean
   [Jean Greenhowe's bazaar bestsellers].
   45 Great gifts to make.
   1. [Jean Greenhowe's bazaar bestsellers].
   II. Title
   745.5

   ISBN 0-7153-9359-6

All rights reserved. No part of this publication may be reproduced, stored in a retrieval system, or transmitted, in any form or by any means, electronic, mechanical, photocopying, recording or otherwise, or any items made for commercial purposes, without the prior permission of David & Charles Publishers plc and the copyright holder.

Designed by Grub Street Design, London

Printed and bound in West Germany
by Mohndruck GmbH
for David & Charles Publishers plc
Brunel House   Newton Abbot   Devon

Distributed in the United States by
Sterling Publishing Co, Inc,
2 Park Avenue, New York, NY 10016

CONTENTS

INTRODUCTION

Here is a bumper collection of gifts which I have designed for *Woman's Weekly* over the years. Space is quite often limited in the magazine and since we do try to cram as much as we can into all our features, it is not always possible to give full-size patterns or as many explanatory diagrams as we would wish. So it has been a great pleasure for me to revise completely all the material for this book, adding full-size patterns, lots of extra diagrams and dozens of useful little tips. There are only a couple of designs where the pattern pieces are so large that they are scaled down onto grids, all the others are printed full-size for tracing right off the pages.

I hope this splendid variety of things to make will be of help in raising funds for your favourite charity. Whatever your sewing skills there is something here for you. The majority of the designs cost next to nothing and are quick and easy to make, but I have also included a few more elaborate features which would be suitable for that extra special gift, or just to keep for yourself.

GENERAL TECHNIQUES

*I*t is worth taking a little time to read through all the preliminary details which follow and also the instructions for each design before you start to make it, so as to be familiar with what is involved.

EQUIPMENT AND MATERIALS

Sewing equipment
Only the usual items which are used for general sewing are required – sewing-machine, sewing threads, sharp scissors (large and small pairs), sewing needles, tape measure, etc. Sewing threads are only mentioned occasionally in the materials specified for each design, when particular colours are necessary for working facial features or other details.

Ruler and yardstick
Use a ruler marked with metric or imperial measurements (whichever you prefer) for measuring and also for tracing the straight edges of patterns off the page or drawing straight lines onto fabric.

If you have a yardstick, this will come in handy for drawing extra long lines, but alternatively a long strip of wood or card will serve the same purpose.

Compasses
You will need a pair of compasses for drawing circles because there are so many used in the various designs. Compasses which are sold for ordinary school use can be purchased at little cost.

Flexible curve
This wonderful little gadget (see the diagram below) is exactly like a flexible ruler.

Designers and draughtsmen use the curve to enable them to draw smooth curved lines which would be impossible free-hand. You will find it invaluable when tracing the curved edges of patterns off the page. Bend it so that the long edge is level with the line, then draw along the edge, just like using a ruler.

If the curve you are drawing is a very tight one, then draw it a bit at a time, moving the flexible curve each

time. Flexible curves can be obtained from retail outlets which sell school and office stationery or artist and designer materials. The one I have is 32cm (12¾in) long and was not expensive.

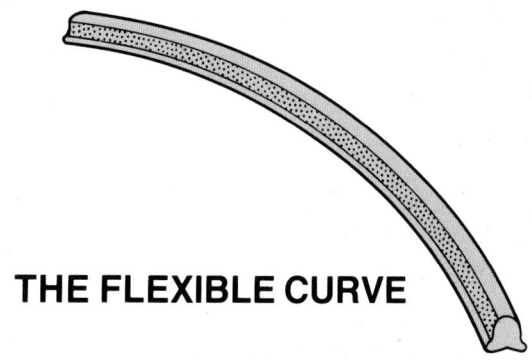

THE FLEXIBLE CURVE

Old scissors
When cutting paper and card, always use a pair of old scissors kept just for this purpose. Never cut these materials with dressmaking and needlework scissors, because paper and card will quickly blunt the blades, making them useless for cutting fabric.

Large pins
Large glass or plastic-headed pins are much better to work with than ordinary dressmaking pins because they are easier to see and handle.

If you are making something for a child, start with a limited number of pins and count them when you are finished, to make sure you have not left any in the fabric.

Leather punch
Although a punch is not essential, it is worth while investing in one if you make a lot of small dolls or animals. The punch can be used to stamp out perfect tiny circles of felt for the eyes and noses. Note that the felt should be treated first with glue as described in the section on adhesive (p. 9).

Tweezers
A pair of pointed or narrow-ended tweezers can be very useful when handling small pieces of felt or trimmings and also to assist in turning very small pieces right side out after stitching.

IMPERIAL (inches)

METRIC (centimetres)

Craft knife

An inexpensive craft knife with a sharp blade is useful for cutting card and also for slitting open cardboard boxes at the corners before cutting out any pieces which may be required.

Graph paper

This is only required for two of the designs (Christmas Stockings and Guard Dog), where the pattern pieces are so large that they have been scaled down onto a grid.

Metric graph paper can be purchased in Britain from shops which stock dressmaking materials, or from haberdashery departments.

Both these designs have to be scaled up onto 5cm (2in) squared paper and, if desired, you can rule a piece of paper into squares of this size instead of buying graph paper.

To copy the patterns from the gridded diagrams, follow the shapes drawn in each gridded square, marking the same shapes onto each square of the graph paper or ruled paper.

Strong thread

This is occasionally required for gathering, when the gathers in thick fabrics or stuffed shapes have to be pulled up very tightly. Buttonhole thread is the type to use. Although this is available in various colours, it is not necessary to have thread which matches the fabric if it will be covered eventually by other materials or trimmings. White is best for general purposes.

Stuffing

There are many types of man-made fibre filling available for toy-making which are suitable for the designs in this book, and all of them are washable. To give some idea of the variety, here is a list from a current catalogue (see list of stockists). All these fillings conform to British standards for health and safety.

De-luxe A siliconed white polyester fibre which gives a luxurious soft touch. Very light and springy with tremendous bulk, this fibre is ideal for top quality toys and makes cushions with a feather-feel.
Super Top-grade white polyester fibre with enormous bulk. Very springy and soft, again for top-grade toys.
Standard A consistent white, crimped polyester with plenty of bounce and bulk.
Economy White polyfibre, fills soft but firm.
Pastel polyester A new, very high bulk, crimped polyester fibre, soft but very bouncy, which has very nearly double the filling capacity of the standard filling. The pretty pastel green fibre is suitable for filling all but a completely white toy, using only half the usual amount.

I like to use the best quality de-luxe for all my projects whether large or small, and although this filling is the most expensive it has very high bulk and so it goes a lot further than cheaper fillings. However, any of the man-made fibre types are preferable to kapok which is messy to work with and cannot be washed, or foam chips which are dangerous.

Such small amounts of filling are needed for most of the designs that cost-wise it will make little difference whichever you use.

Cotton wool is specified for some items and this should be the kind which comes in rolls or folded like a concertina. Cotton-wool balls could also be used if you tease them out first with your fingers.

There are several bean-bags in the book and when they were designed I filled them with dried lentils. At the time this was the only suitable filling and traditionally all such items were filled with dried beans. The only drawback is that although these bean-bags are safe enough for older children to play with, they cannot be washed.

However, commercially made plastic granules are now available which conform to British safety standards. You can obtain these by post from The Handicraft Shop (see list of stockists).

Card

Three types only are required, all of which are likely to be found around the house.

When thin strong card is mentioned, this is the kind you can cut from breakfast cereal packets, washing-powder packets, and so on.

The second type is corrugated reinforced card, as used for the strong boxes in which manufacturers send their products in bulk to shops and supermarkets. The corrugated reinforcing is always contained between layers of strong paper (most often brown), so you can only actually see the corrugations at the edges of the card. Although this card will bend easily at each of the corrugations, if you glue two layers together with the corrugations running in opposite directions, it becomes quite rigid.

Extremely thin flexible card is sometimes needed and for this you can cut up old Christmas and greetings cards, which are about the right thickness. Each particular type of card required is always quoted in the instructions.

Adhesive

I like UHU all-purpose adhesive for sticking practically everything because it dries so quickly, but you can use whatever you prefer so long as it is suitable for the material which is to be stuck.

When cutting out small felt shapes, the cut edges do tend to be rather hairy because felt is composed of fibres which are compressed together and the fibres shed at the edges.

To counteract this, first spread one surface of the felt with adhesive, work it into the felt with a fingertip, then leave to dry. Take care not to use too much glue, or it will soak through to the other side of the felt. When the glue is dry, place an old cloth on your ironing board to protect it, then press the right side of the felt with a steam iron or hot iron over a damp cloth. When you cut the pieces from felt treated in this way, the cut edges will be much smoother. This method should not be used on felt pieces which are to be stitched and stuffed, of course.

To remove the odd unwanted smear of UHU on fabric, felt or trimmings, use a bit of cloth dipped in acetone and dab until the acetone dissolves and removes the glue. Take care when using acetone as it is highly flammable. You can get it from any pharmacist shop.

I also use UHU to neaten the cut edges of braid, ribbon and lace edging to stop the edges from fraying. Spread a little adhesive on the wrong side and leave to dry before cutting. If adding a ribbon bow to a design, leave the ends a little longer than necessary and spread the back of the ribbon ends with a little glue before cutting to the required length.

Ordinary shoe-lace and sports shoe-lace can be sealed in the same way. These laces are usually tubular in construction so you can open the ends by pushing in a pencil point, dot a little glue inside, then press the raw edges together. When the glue is dry, trim off the ragged ends.

If working continuously with a tube of adhesive it is a nuisance to have to keep screwing on the lid, so stand the tube upright in an old mug or cup between gluing operations to prevent leakage.

Copydex adhesive is mentioned in one of the designs, but any latex-based type glue will do.

Shoe-laces

Ordinary shoe-laces and sports shoe-laces can be used for inexpensive decorations and trimmings. The sports-shoe type is a bit wider than the ordinary lace and it comes in extremely long lengths and bright colours for lacing up training shoes and football boots.

Fur fabric

You should be able to get the required fur fabrics quite easily, but mail order suppliers are listed at the end of the book. If a particular kind is not specified in the instructions, then use the ordinary short-pile type.

On fur fabrics, the fur pile lies smooth and flat if stroked in one direction along the length and will lift up if stroked in the opposite direction. Always cut out the pieces with the smooth stroke of the fur pile following the direction of the arrows on the pattern pieces.

To cut out fur fabric, pin the patterns to the *wrong* side of the fabric, then snip through the back surface of the fabric carefully a bit at a time. If you take large scissor strokes (as you would with other fabrics), then you will chop off bits of pile on the right side, resulting in ugly bald patches on the finished item.

Always cut fur fabric pieces singly, never from double fabric, and take care to reverse the pattern for the *second* piece when a pair of pieces is required.

After stitching the seams, tease out the fur pile trapped in the seams with the point of a needle or pin.

Fleecy fabric is also required for some designs and it is available from dress-fabric shops for making dressing-gowns, etc. It has a knitted backing like the other fur fabrics, but it is brushed on the right side to form a soft furry surface. It does not have a long pile like the other fur fabrics.

Velcro fastener

This is sold by the centimetre or inch and is available from fabric shops and haberdashery departments in a variety of colours.

Velcro is composed of two flat narrow nylon strips, one strip has hundreds of tiny hooks and the other has a furry surface composed of minute loops. When the strips are pressed firmly together the hooks catch in the loops and the strips cannot be pulled apart sideways. However, they can be separated simply by peeling them apart.

Iron-on interfacing

Sometimes called interlining, this non-woven type of fabric is used in dressmaking to add firmness or stiffening to collars and facings. It is bonded onto the wrong side of the fabric by ironing. Interfacing is sold by the metre or yard and is available from dress-fabric shops in light, medium and firm weights. There are two colours only, white for light coloured fabrics and grey for darker shades.

Coloured pencils and marker pens

When coloured pencils are quoted, these should be the ordinary type of pencil used for colouring, *not* wax crayons. I use an orangy-red shade to colour the cheeks on dolls and animals. Rub the *side* of the pencil lead on the fabric when colouring cheeks. This works well on some fabrics, but for others you may need to moisten the pencil tip slightly.

Marker pens should always be the permanent kind, not water-based.

Fabrics and trimmings

Pretty fabrics and trimmings are all-important for bazaar makes and even the simplest of designs can look quite stunning if you choose the materials carefully. Such small pieces of fabric are required for most of the designs that you can even use expensive materials such as Liberty Tana lawn at little cost. Outlets which stock this fabric are quite used to selling very small quantities such as 10cm (⅛yd), for making patchwork.

Ribbons, trimmings and printed cotton fabrics can often be bought in street markets more cheaply than in shops and if you buy these as and when you see them, then you will build up a stock for future use.

If you have a rag-bag, then there are sure to be some dressmaking cuttings or cast-off garments which could be of use. It is also worth looking out for any suitable nearly-new garments at jumble sales and in thrift shops. These can usually be purchased at a fraction of what you would pay for the fabric itself and an enormous number of lavender sachets could be made from one pretty printed blouse, for example.

If working with multi-coloured printed fabrics, use complementary colours for your trimmings, for example a red ribbon bow to pick out the red in the print. A neat finish is important also. Don't have any ends of sewing thread sticking out and neaten the cut ends of ribbon or trimming as described in the section on adhesive.

GENERAL INSTRUCTIONS

Measurements

All sizes are given in metric, with the imperial measurements in brackets. During the designing process I work out each measurement individually, to suit both metric and imperial, and you will notice that sets of measurements do not always convert in exactly the same way. I often round them off to avoid an awkward size, for example a straight strip of fabric 13cm in length should convert accurately to 5⅛in. If the ⅛in will make no difference whatsoever to the finished item, then it is rounded down to 5in. All such inconsistencies are deliberate and not printing errors. Simply stick to metric or imperial throughout each design, whichever you prefer.

Where the quantities of material required are concerned, I may quote that you need 25cm of fabric and convert this to the nearest 10in instead of giving the yardage in which it could be purchased – ⅜yd or 13½in. This is done to save wastage, so that if making more than one item you can double or treble the amount specified and *then* buy the nearest yardage.

Copying the patterns

For tracing the patterns off the page, use ordinary plain white paper such as that used in inexpensive jotting pads, or the cheapest typing paper. Just make sure that the pattern outlines are visible through the paper. I always use typing paper for my patterns and they withstand repeated use. When they get a bit holey from constant pinning, they can be repaired with bits of sticky tape.

Tracing paper is not really suitable for patterns as it is too crisp to be pinned many times without tearing.

To trace the patterns off the page, first fix the paper securely to the page with tiny bits of reusable adhesive putty, such as Sticky Tack or Blue Tack. Trace the straight lines with a ruler and the curves with a flexible curve, as described. You can trace curves free-hand by drawing them a bit at a time, but this takes a little longer.

Trace off completely circular patterns with compasses, putting your compass point at the centre dot shown on the pattern.

Mark all details onto the pattern pieces, then remove the paper from the page and cut out the patterns.

Some patterns have to be traced onto folded paper because you will only be able to get a perfectly symmetrical shape this way. You should do this as follows.

Fold a piece of paper in half, making sure that it is large enough for both halves to cover the complete area of the pattern. Crease the fold sharply. Now open up the folded paper, having the outer sharp edge of fold uppermost. Flatten the fold.

Place this folded edge along the line indicated on the pattern, then secure paper to page with bits of putty. Trace off the pattern outline onto the paper. Remove the paper from the page and refold it, making sure your pattern outline is on the outside.

You now have to cut out the pattern through both thicknesses and this can be a bit tricky as the two paper layers tend to slip apart as you cut, especially if the pattern is a large one. To counteract this, open up the folded paper slightly and put dots of glue on the inside, just *outside* the area of the pattern outline. The drawn line is easy to see if you hold it up to a strong light.

Now press the paper layers together and they will stay together as you cut out the pattern. Unfold the paper and you have the complete pattern.

Rectangular patterns

Where measurements are quoted for a particular piece, these can be marked with ruler and pencil straight onto the wrong side of the fabric. However, if you are making the design many times, cut paper patterns to the measurements given, so that you don't have to

measure each time. Remember to mark details on the pattern so that you will know what it is for the next time you use it.

Circular patterns

There are so many circles required throughout the book that I have included a handy rule (see p. 8), marked in centimetres and inches, which you can use to set your compasses to.

Circle measurements are always given as the diameter, that is, the distance across the centre of the circle, and you should set your compasses to half this measurement.

For example, if you need a circle 10cm (4in) in diameter, set the distance between the compass point and pencil tip to 5cm (2in), then draw the circle onto paper.

Where a circle is included on the page as one of the patterns for a design, there is always a dot marking the centre so that you can trace it using compasses instead of trying to do it free-hand.

Don't throw away your paper circles after making a design because they will certainly be of use for others. Remember to mark on the centre point (this is sometimes needed to mark the fabric) and also write on the diameter size.

Cutting, stitching and marking fabrics

Place all patterns on the straight grain of the fabric unless other instructions are given and pin patterns to the wrong side of the fabric.

Cutting out small felt pieces can be awkward and fiddly, especially if the pattern pieces are too small to pin. In these cases attach the paper pattern to the felt with a dot of glue. Cut out the piece, then peel off the pattern. You can only do this, of course, if the glued side of the felt is to be hidden, for example for eyes and noses.

If any marks have to be transferred onto the fabric from the pattern, keep the pattern pinned to the fabric,

DIAGRAM — showing how to stitch around a paper pattern

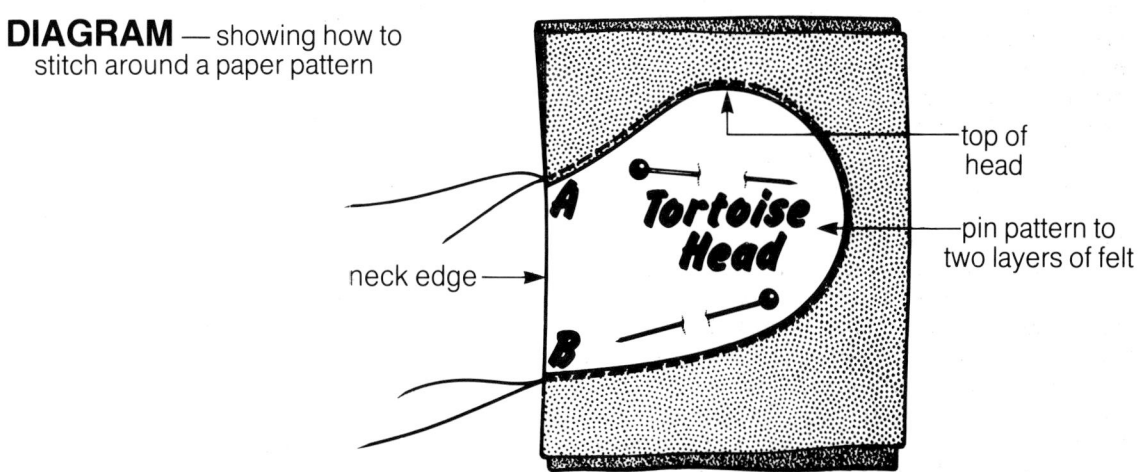

neck edge →

top of head

pin pattern to two layers of felt

then, using a sharp pencil, push the point through the pattern and into the fabric to make a dot. If a line has to be marked, make pencil dots at intervals along the line and at each end, then remove the pattern and join up the dots. Mark centres of circles with dots in the same way.

Join and seam all pieces with right sides together unless otherwise stated. All seam allowances are quoted in the instructions for each design.

Some of the fabric pieces are seamed by pinning the paper pattern to the fabric, then stitching all around level with the edge of the pattern. This is described fully in every case where it is used, but a diagram is included here to explain the process clearly. The diagram on (p. 11) shows the stitching of the tortoise's head (see Tiny Tortoises, p. 62).

For this method, you may need to use ordinary dressmaking pins for holding the patterns to the fabric, especially if dealing with small patterns.

When you are fastening off the thread after hand-sewing, do not snip it off near to the fastening off, but pass the needle back through the fabric and stuffing where you fastened off to come out at a different position. Pull the thread through, then snip it off near to the fabric and the end will disappear back into the stuffing. Leaving a length of thread inside the stuffing will prevent unravelling.

Ladder stitch

This stitch is used for closing the opening on anything which has been turned right side out and stuffed. The raw edges of the fabric are turned in at the seam line, then these seam line edges are laced together from side to side, forming stitches which look like a ladder, as shown in the diagram below.

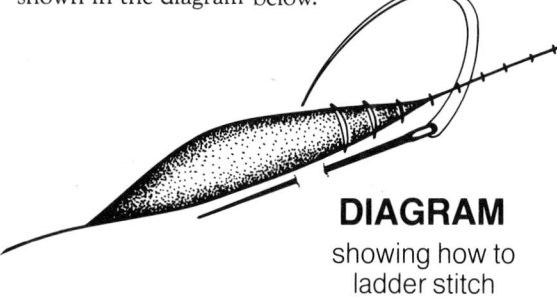

DIAGRAM
showing how to
ladder stitch

Use single, double, or strong thread, according to the thickness of the fabric, and take small straight stitches alternately along one edge of the fabric, then the other. After working a few stitches, pull the thread just tight enough to draw the fabric edges together. If working a long line of stitches, make a small back stitch every so often so that the ladder stitches will not spring open again.

This stitch is also useful for sewing two completely separate pieces together, working stitches in the same way, to join pieces almost invisibly.

Tying ribbon bows

If you are tying a ribbon bow *around* something, then it is useful to know how to make a bow which will sit squarely and not crooked.

First tie a single knot. You will now have one length of ribbon stretching above the knot and the other below it. Use the length of ribbon *below* the knot to make the first loop. Bring the other length down over and under the loop, then complete the bow.

To make an extremely small bow, tie the bow, pinch the tied centre with finger and thumb, then pull the ends of the ribbon with the other hand until the loops are a bit smaller than the size you need. Tug the loops again to tighten the bow. Now trim the ribbon ends to the required length.

How to gather a circle

So many circles are gathered and stuffed throughout the book that it is described here in detail.

The row of gathering stitches should generally be about 3mm (⅛in) within the raw edge of the circle. If the fabric is closely woven this works all right, but on loosely woven fabrics you need to gather a bit further away from the edge or the thread will pull through the raw edge when the gathers are drawn up.

Use double thread or buttonhole thread (according to the thickness of the fabric) and knot the ends together. Take a small stitch to secure knot near to the edge of the circle, then take a small back stitch at this position also, so that the knot will not slip through the fabric when you pull the gathers tight.

Take small running stitches all around the circle, finishing a little beyond where you started. If the fabric is thick, then take larger stitches. Pull up the gathers, stuffing the circle as you do this, while holding tightly onto the thread near to the gathers. Pull up until the raw edges meet.

Now hold tightly onto the thread beside the gathers with the finger and thumb of one hand, while you take a back stitch through the gathers with a needle and thread in your other hand. Pull the needle and thread up tightly, only relaxing your grip on the thread at the very last second. Oversew several times through the fabric to secure.

When the instructions say to pull up gathers tightly this always means until the raw edges meet, unless otherwise stated.

A production line

If you are making any design in quantity, then it is easier and much quicker to set up a production line instead of making and finishing each article individually.

You can cut out several pieces in one operation by pinning the pattern to a few layers of fabric, depending on the thickness. Do all the cutting out first, then the stitching, then stuff all the pieces at the same time. Finally, add any trimmings.

BRILLIANT BANGLES, BRIGHT BEADS

Nothing could be made more cheaply than this exciting array of pretty things. Just save some plastic lemonade bottles, carrier-bags and wastepaper and you can conjure up a whole collection of jewellery from junk.

Although it is hard to believe, clear plastic food-bags when plaited make the most glamorous of bracelets and those bits of old wallpaper and gift wrapping you have stored away for no good reason can be used at last – to create strings of beads.

The transparent bangles are a bit more expensive, costing at least a few pence each. They are put together in minutes, from plastic siphon tubing which you can fill with lots of different things.

PAPER BEADS

I experimented with virtually every type of paper when making the beads, even newspaper. They all resulted in strong rigid beads, when made in the following manner. The barrel-shaped type of bead works best, made from a tapered strip of paper rolled up from the widest end. The secret of making strong beads is not to taper the full length of the strip, but to leave about one third of it straight. When rolled up, this straight portion gives the bead a rigid centre core, so that it cannot be bent or crushed.

When choosing paper, remember that only the *edges* of the strip will show when the beads are finished. You should experiment, because the results can be quite surprising and unexpected. Cuttings from magazines will give a random effect which can be most unusual and beads made from brown wrapping-paper or envelopes when varnished, resemble wood.

Gift wrapping-paper also makes good beads. The pink and gold beads in the necklace illustrated in the colour photograph were made from pink paper which had a zigzag design. To complement this, I made the smaller gold beads from a bit of metallic foil wrapping-paper. Foil should be the paper-backed type or you won't be able to glue it. In the same way, kitchen foil is not suitable.

Thick papers, like wallpaper, will make super chunky ridged beads, thinner papers make thin, smooth beads.

For the green necklace and the pendant, I used thick wallpaper for the large beads and cuttings off a golden brown envelope as well as plain green paper for the others. All were varnished. The pendant illustrates that you don't have to make a lot of beads. One really chunky bead with a few tiny ones is just as effective.

You can use any kind of adhesive that will stick paper. UHU is good because it dries very quickly, but take care not to get it on the right side of the paper. You only need a dot or two of adhesive – it's not necessary to cover the whole length of the strip.

If your paper is shiny, then leave the beads as they are. If matt paper is used, then a coat of clear nail-varnish will protect and brighten the colours.

To varnish the beads, hold each one on the pointed end of a knitting-needle which is a bit larger than the hole in the bead. Brush the bead with varnish, then slip it onto a thinner knitting-needle. Prop up the needle at each end (you can use two cup or mug handles) and leave them to dry.

Specific instructions are given for the necklaces illustrated, so that the process of making can be completely described. But do experiment for yourself. Have fun!

GENERAL BEAD-MAKING INSTRUCTIONS

You will need: Paper as suggested; cord, string or knitting yarn for threading the beads; a No 10 (3¼mm, USA: 3) knitting-needle for forming the beads; adhesive; clear nail-varnish (optional); pencil; ruler; a long strip of wood or card (yardstick if you have one) for ruling lines on paper; scissors for cutting paper (*not* your best dressmaking scissors – paper will blunt them).

To cut out the paper strips

Decide on the *length* of the finished bead, then rule your paper into strips, making the *width* of the strips this measurement. Always rule lines on the wrong side of the paper.

Now mark another line *across* the paper at right

angles to the others, about a third of the way down the length. Starting from this line, rule two lines, to taper each strip to about 3mm (⅛in) at the end as shown in Diagram 1. The first strip is shown shaded in the diagram, for clarity. Continue ruling every strip to taper it as before, then cut out all strips, discarding the smaller tapered bits in between.

To form each bead

Place the knitting-needle across the wrong side of the untapered end of one paper strip and roll the strip firmly once around the needle. Dab a little adhesive across the strip and roll up a little more, using one hand to turn the needle and the other to steady the rolled up strip. Before continuing, check that the bead can be slipped along the needle for removing when completed.

Continue rolling up the strip, dabbing a little glue for a few inches at a time down the centre of the strip, until the bead is completed (see Diagram 2). Make sure that the tapered end is securely stuck in place, then slip the bead off the needle and leave it to dry.

Pink and gold necklace

I made 19 pink beads, cutting 2.5cm (1in) wide strips by the full length of the wrapping-paper; also 32 gold beads from strips 1×60cm (⅜×24in), tapering the strips for *half* the length to make them a bit more chunky.

This necklace has a double strand of alternate pink and gold beads at the front, which join into a single strand of gold beads at the back of the neck. It is threaded as follows. Thread 8 pink and 7 gold beads alternately onto a length of cord, beginning and ending with a pink bead. In the same way, thread 9 pink and 8 gold beads onto another length of cord.

Thread the ends of *both* cords at each end of the strings of beads, through 1 gold, then 1 pink bead. Finally, thread 7 gold beads onto double cords at each end. There is now one gold bead left over, which is to be used for the fastening.

To make the fastening

First join the two cords by sewing them together at each end of necklace with sewing thread. Trim off one cord only, at each end near to the join. Thread the remaining gold bead onto one of the cords, then loop the cord back on itself around the bead. Sew around the double cord to hold the bead in place. Trim off excess length of cord, but leave enough length to pass back through the last two threaded gold beads.

Make a loop on the remaining cord at the other end of the necklace, large enough to pass over the bead. Sew around the double cord to hold the loop in place. Before trimming off any excess length, use cord to make a knot at sewn base of loop, so that the beads will not slip off. Finish off cord as for other end.

Brown and green necklace

For this, I made 3 large beads from green patterned wallpaper, 33 small from brown paper and 6 from green paper, threaded onto a single cord. All the beads were varnished.

Thread on 15 brown, 1 green, 1 large, 1 green, 1 brown, 1 green, 1 large, 1 green, 1 brown, 1 green, 1 large, 1 green and 15 brown. Use the remaining brown bead to make a fastening as for the pink and gold necklace.

The pendant necklace

Diagram 3 shows the pendant bead. This necklace was made from the same wallpaper and brown paper as the green necklace. All the beads were varnished.

To make the tapered pendant shape, cut a 5×100cm (2×39in) strip. Leave about a quarter of the strip straight, then cut one long edge of the remainder only, tapering it towards the long edge at the other end of the strip. Make 6 small brown beads.

Thread one small bead onto a length of cord, then pass both ends of cord through the pendant bead and also 1 small bead. Thread 2 small beads onto each end of cord.

I left the cord long enough to pass over the head, knotting the ends together, but you can make a fastening if desired, as for the other necklaces.

TUBULAR BANGLES

The transparent plastic siphon tubing used for these bangles is obtainable from shops which sell home-brewing equipment. You should shop around, as prices vary considerably. I found the best buy at Boots where the tubing is sold in 2.5m (2¾yd) lengths. You can make nine or ten adult-sized bracelets from this length, working out at just a few pence each.

The tubing can be filled with anything you can think of and here are a few examples which I used for the bangles illustrated.

Gold or silver glitter (loose, as used for decoration at Christmas). Lentils (you could try other foods such as coloured sugar or desiccated coconut). Silver beads – my beads were large enough to fill the centre diameter of the tubing, so they made a *row* of beads; you could also use seed beads or sugar strands or hundreds and thousands as used for cake decoration.

Plastic net bag (the type which fruit and vegetables are sold in), inserting it into the tubing with a thin knitting-needle pushed against the sealed base of the bag. Gold tinsel (the miniature kind which is bound onto a central wire, rather like a pipe-cleaner). Strands of coloured plastic - covered wire (electrical), coiled tightly around a knitting-needle, removed from needle, then stretched apart slightly before inserting into tubing.

You will need: Siphon tubing; fillings as suggested; cuttings off a transparent plastic lemonade or other drinks bottle, for making the join; oddment of gold or silver paper-backed foil wrapping-paper, for covering the join; sticky tape; adhesive; a sharp craft knife or penknife; a pair of pointed tweezers.

To make

If you are making the bangle for yourself, cut a narrow strip of thin card and join the ends to make a bangle shape. Try it on – it should be just large enough to push over your hand, but not loose enough to fall off.

Otherwise, for an average-size bracelet, cut a 24cm (9½in) length of tubing, using the craft knife and keeping your cut as straight as possible.

The cut ends of the tubing are held together with a little coil of plastic made from a strip cut off the lemonade bottle. Cut the strip to size indicated in the pattern – you don't need to be too precise about this, but take care to cut the strip so that the curve of plastic (*around* the bottle) goes in the direction shown.

To roll up the strip, grip one short end with tweezers and roll it up very tightly along the length as shown on the pattern. Holding firmly onto the tweezers and the rolled up strip, push *half* of it into one end of the tube. Release your grip and remove the tweezers. The strip will uncoil to grip the inside of the tube firmly. Diagram 4 shows the coil in position with the remaining half left protruding, for joining on the other end of the tube.

Now insert the filling in the other open end of the tube. If you are using loose fillings, such as glitter, put a bit of sticky tape over the end of the plastic coil to prevent any material falling through. Spoon in the filling, working over a basin to catch any over-spills.

After filling, remove sticky tape if used, then ease the other open end of the tube over the protruding half of the coiled up plastic strip, so that the ends of the tube meet. Cut a bit of sticky tape the same size as the plastic strip, and wind it around the bangle at the join. Once this joining process is done, the ends of the tubing should be so securely held together that you should not be able to pull them apart. Test this to be sure.

To cover the sticky tape, cut a strip of silver or gold paper as for the plastic strip, making it a fraction wider. Glue it around the sticky tape. Burnish the paper strip by rubbing with a polishing cloth.

BRIGHT BRACELETS

Although not designed to last forever, these cheap and cheerful bracelets are all really easy to make from plastic food-bags, carrier-bags, wrapping-paper and plastic bottles. Detailed instructions are given for each bracelet illustrated, but you can use your own ideas, once you know how they are made.

PLAITED BRACELET

You will need: Three 24×40cm (9½×15¾in) plastic food-bags; sticky tape; a bit of 2.5cm (1in) wide silver braid or ribbon; adhesive.

To make

Cut the sealed side edges off the plastic bags so that they can be opened up into three long strips of plastic. Gather them all tightly together at one end and bind around a bit of sticky tape. Secure this end to the edge of a table with sticky tape.

Now plait the three strips, at the same time giving each strip two twists away from you before plaiting. When you have plaited about 8cm (3in), hold on to one of the strips firmly while pushing the plait back on itself as far as it will go (this is fascinating).

Continue plaiting and pushing back in the same way while holding onto the same strip (you will know which strip because it will be longer than the others). When the plait is completed, bind the ends together with sticky tape as before and trim off the longer end.

Overlap the bound ends of the plait and press tightly to flatten. Bind with sticky tape. Glue braid around the join, winding it round several times.

YELLOW BRACELET

You will need: A plastic lemonade (or other) bottle; a thin soft carrier-bag; sticky tape.

To make

Use sharp scissors to cut away the base and upper shaped portion of the bottle. Cut open the remaining tube-shaped piece along the length of the bottle. Flatten the plastic piece, curved side down, on a table. Use a darning needle and ruler to draw a 2.5cm (1in) wide strip across the width (the curve going *around* the bottle).

Cut out the strip and form it into a bracelet of the required size, overlapping the ends as necessary and securing the ends with sticky tape.

Cut your plastic bag into strips about 5cm (2in) wide, making them as long as possible. You can make a continuous strip by cutting in a spiral, working from the top of the bag down towards the bottom. Any designs or lettering on the carrier-bag will form an attractive decoration.

Secure one end of the strip inside the bracelet with sticky tape. Now bind the strip tightly around the plastic bracelet, creasing the plastic as you go. When completely covered, secure the end of the strip with a bit of sticky tape on the inside of the bracelet.

PINK AND WHITE BRACELET

I made this from a more up-market type of carrier-bag, which was firmer and stiffer than the one used for the yellow bracelet. It is made in the same basic way.

Make the basic shape as for the yellow bracelet, using a 2cm (¾in) wide strip cut off the plastic bottle. Before covering with the carrier-bag strip, pad the bracelet by binding it with strips cut off a pedal-bin liner.

For the outer cover, cut the bag into 2cm (¾in) wide strips. Fold them in half along the length, printed side outside. Bind around the bracelet evenly, keeping the plastic strip smooth and having the folded edges showing as you go. Secure the ends with sticky tape as before.

GOLD BRACELET

I used gold foil hologram wrapping-paper for this, which looks really gorgeous. To make the basic bracelet a bit thicker, cut three strips off the plastic bottle, any width you like.

Make one strip into the desired size of bracelet, but instead of overlapping the ends, trim them to length and butt the ends together, securing with sticky tape. Repeat this with the other two strips inside the first strip, having the joins at different positions, so that the bracelet is perfectly rounded.

Now cut paper strips and bind the bracelet in the same way as given for the pink bracelet. Secure the ends on the inside with sticky tape as before.

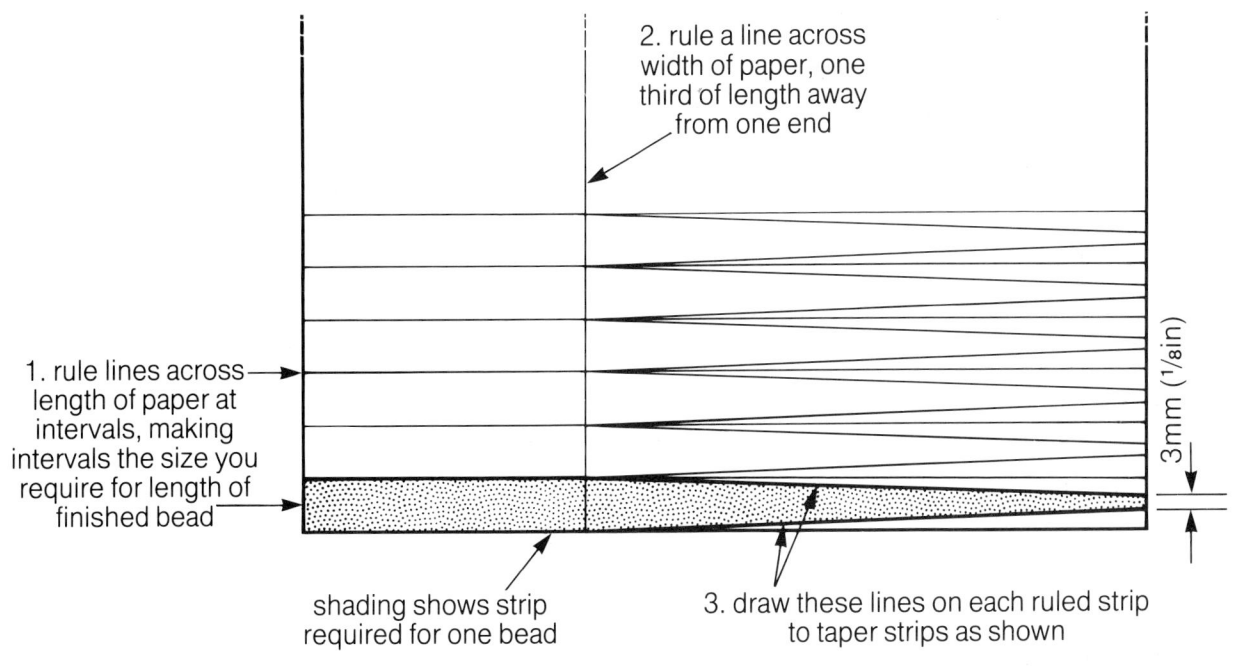

2. rule a line across width of paper, one third of length away from one end

1. rule lines across length of paper at intervals, making intervals the size you require for length of finished bead

3mm (1/8in)

shading shows strip required for one bead

3. draw these lines on each ruled strip to taper strips as shown

DIAGRAM 1 — showing how to cut paper strips for the bead

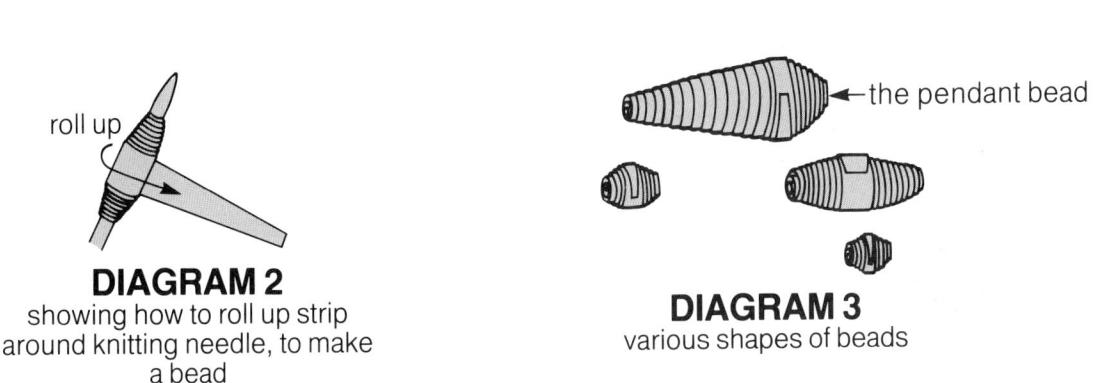

roll up

DIAGRAM 2
showing how to roll up strip around knitting needle, to make a bead

the pendant bead

DIAGRAM 3
various shapes of beads

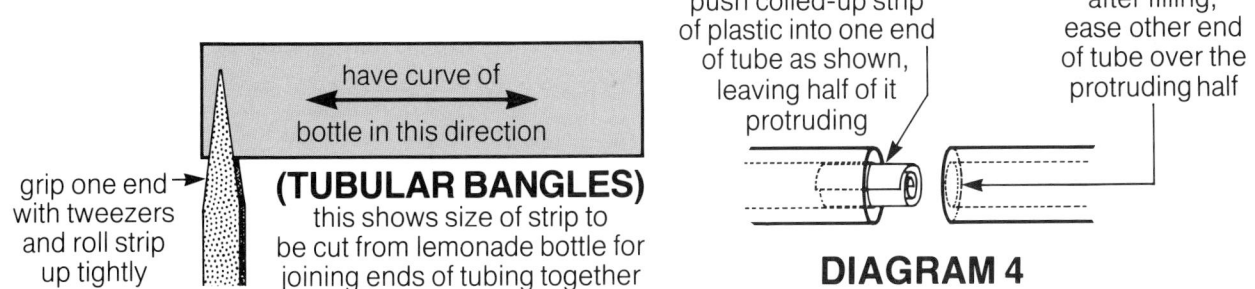

have curve of bottle in this direction

(TUBULAR BANGLES)
this shows size of strip to be cut from lemonade bottle for joining ends of tubing together

grip one end with tweezers and roll strip up tightly

push coiled-up strip of plastic into one end of tube as shown, leaving half of it protruding

after filling, ease other end of tube over the protruding half

DIAGRAM 4

NOVELTY SKIPPING-ROPES

Designed to appeal to children of all ages, these skipping-rope handles look good enough to eat. The same basic cone shape is used for both sets of handles which measure roughly 12.5cm (5in) in length.

The ice-cream cone effect is achieved by placing wide mesh rug canvas over peach-coloured felt. I chose pink crushed velvet for the ice-cream topping, but white fabric could be used instead.

You will need: Small pieces of: orange and peach-coloured felt, pink or white fabric, wide mesh rug canvas; a few strands green knitting yarn; clothes-line rope (a 1.5m (1⅝yd) length is about right for a small child); strong thread; cotton wool for stuffing; permanent fine-tipped black marker pen.

Notes: Patterns are given full-size and 5mm (¼in) seams are allowed. If you have any difficulty getting the rug canvas, wide mesh curtain net would make a good alternative.

To make the rope with carrot handles
For each handle, cut one piece from orange felt, placing

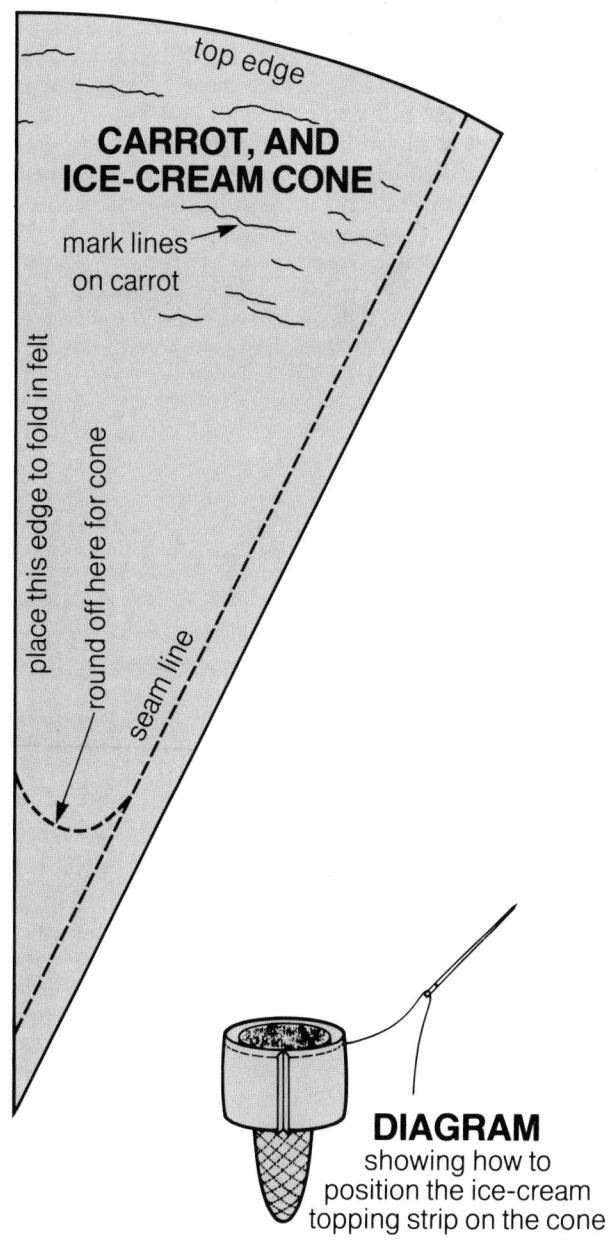

top edge

CARROT, AND
ICE-CREAM CONE

mark lines
on carrot

place this edge to fold in felt

round off here for cone

seam line

DIAGRAM
showing how to
position the ice-cream
topping strip on the cone

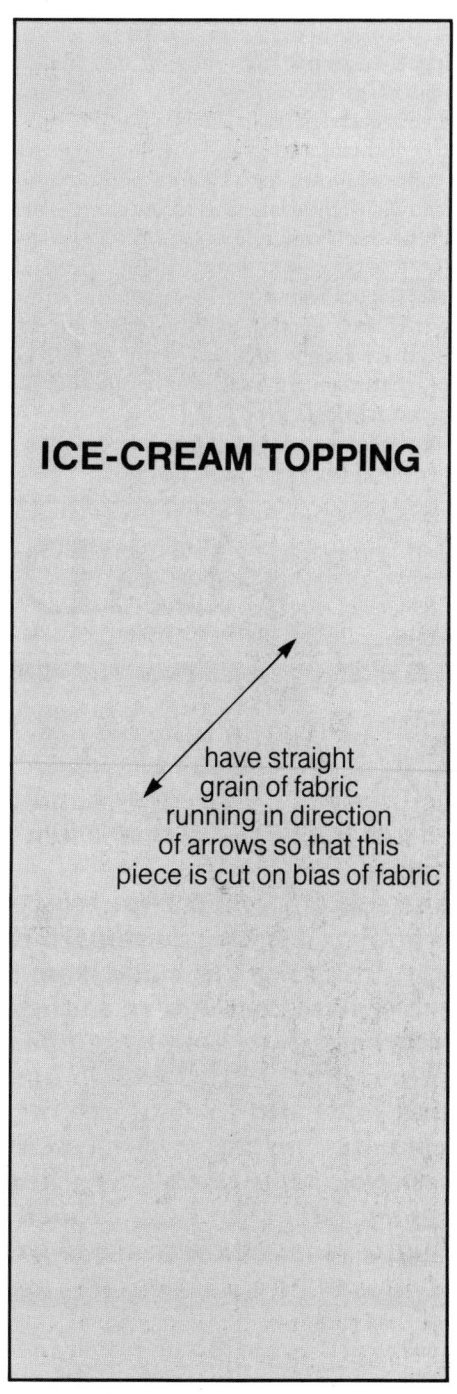

ICE-CREAM TOPPING

have straight
grain of fabric
running in direction
of arrows so that this
piece is cut on bias of fabric

edge of pattern indicated to fold in felt. Open up the felt pieces and, using a black pen, mark the lines here and there all over, as shown on the upper portion of the pattern. Press felt pieces with a hot iron over a paper tissue to make sure marked lines are quite dry.

Join the edges of each piece at seam line shown on the pattern. Turn right side out, stuff firmly with cotton wool, then run a strong gathering thread around top edge. Cut the required length of rope and make a knot at each end. Slip knots inside gathered edges of carrots together with folded ends of a few folded strands of knitting yarn. Pull up gathering threads tightly and fasten off. Sew through the gathers, the rope and strands of yarn to hold them securely.

oddment of plain fabric for covering the cone. Cut out fabric 2cm (¾in) larger all round than the paper pattern. Now wrap this piece around cardboard cone, having wrong side outside. Pin straight edges together to make the fabric piece fit the cone snugly, taking care that curved edge of fabric extends beyond lower edge of cone. Remove fabric and stitch seam as pinned.

Trim seam, then turn piece right side out. Replace it over the cone, then turn and glue extra fabric at lower edge to inside of cone, keeping fabric taut as you do this.

For the base, cut a 12cm (4¾in) diameter circle of

card and check to see that this fits the base of your cone. If not, adjust circle to fit. Place card circle on a piece of the same kind of fabric as used for covering the cone, then cut out fabric 2cm (¾in) larger all round. Gather around the edge of this circle, place card circle at centre, then pull up gathers tightly to the other side of the card and fasten off.

Place circle in position at base of cone, having gathers on inside, then oversew edges of fabrics together. To neaten, glue a length of lace trimming around lower edge of cone.

The arms

Cut a straight 32cm (12½in) length of wire off the coat-hanger. Pierce a small hole through the cone, from one side to the other, 4cm (1⅝in) down from top of cone. Push the wire through, having it protruding an equal amount at each side. Cut two narrow bias strips from an oddment of fabric. Use these to secure wire to cone by binding and gluing it around a portion of wire at each side of cone, then around the cone itself, as shown in Diagram 2.

Now bend 2.5cm (1in) at each end of the wire back on itself to form the hands as shown in Diagram 2. Bend each wire arm down a little at each side of cone for slope of shoulders, then bend up again half-way along the length to form the elbows as shown in the diagram.

Pad the hands and arms by wrapping a little cotton wool around the wire, securing it to the wire by winding round lengths of sewing thread.

Cut four hand pieces from flesh-coloured felt and join them in pairs, taking a 3mm (⅛in) seam and leaving wrist edges open. Trim seams and turn hands right side out. Slip the felt hands in position over ends of wire, taking care not to push back the cotton-wool padding.

The bodice

Only the front portion of the cone needs to be covered, the rest will be hidden by the shawl. Cut the bodice piece from the same type of fabric which you wish to use for the sleeves. Glue it around the front of the cone as directed on the bodice pattern, keeping it smooth against the cone.

The skirt

Fold the skirt fabric in half, bringing the 46cm (18in) edges together and having the right side of the fabric outside. Press as folded, then tack all the raw edges together.

Turn the folded edge of the fabric up 10cm (4in) and press as shown in Diagram 3. This doubled portion will form the deepest skirt pockets. Mark the *pocket* fabric layers with a pin near to top edge as shown in the diagram to ensure that you will stitch the lace trimming to the correct edge when the fabric is unfolded.

Unfold pocket, then stitch lace trimming to top edge of pocket as marked. Fold the pocket in position again.

Now fold up and press the lower edge of fabric once more, but this time only 2cm (¾in), to form the shallow skirt pockets, as shown in Diagram 4. Mark with a pin, unfold and stitch lace trimming to top of this pocket as before.

Fold both pockets in position again and press, then tack through all thicknesses of fabric at the side edges.

To form the separate pocket divisions, stitch through all thicknesses of pockets and skirt fabric at positions shown in Diagram 5. Draw thread ends through to wrong side of skirt and knot.

Now join the short side edges of skirt, taking a 1cm (⅜in) seam and having wrong side outside. Turn skirt right side out. Run a gathering thread around the remaining raw edges. Slip skirt onto doll, having skirt seam at centre back. Pull up gathers tightly around the cone, having lower edge of skirt level with base of cone, then fasten off securely. Space out gathers evenly all round, then glue a piece of ribbon around the cone to cover gathered raw edges of fabric.

The sleeves

For each sleeve cut a 10cm (4in) square of fabric to match the bodice piece. Join two opposite edges of each square, taking a 3mm (⅛in) seam. Turn sleeves right side out.

Turn in each remaining raw edge of each sleeve 3mm (⅛in) and run round gathering threads. Put the sleeves on the arms and pull up one gathered edge tightly around the top of arm next to cone, then fasten off. Pull up other gathers tightly around wrist edges of hands, then fasten off and catch gathers to hands. Glue a bit of lace trimming around gathers on each wrist.

The head

Cut a 10cm (4in) diameter circle of flesh-coloured felt. Gather around edge using double thread. Pull up gathers and stuff head very firmly. Draw gathers up tightly until edges meet, then fasten off. Note that gathers will be at back of doll's head.

Now snip a tiny hole in felt at position shown in Diagram 6. Push pointed end of a pencil inside head at this position, twisting it around and around to open up stuffing so that head may be glued to top of cone.

Spread top of cone with glue, then push head in position, tilting it slightly to one side, as shown in the colour photograph. Leave until glue dries.

You can now shape the chin, by inserting a needle point at the lower edge of face and easing felt and stuffing downwards.

For the eyes, cut two tiny circles of black felt (use leather punch if available) and glue them in place half-way down face and 1cm (⅜in) apart. Work two small stitches in black thread at top of each eye to form the

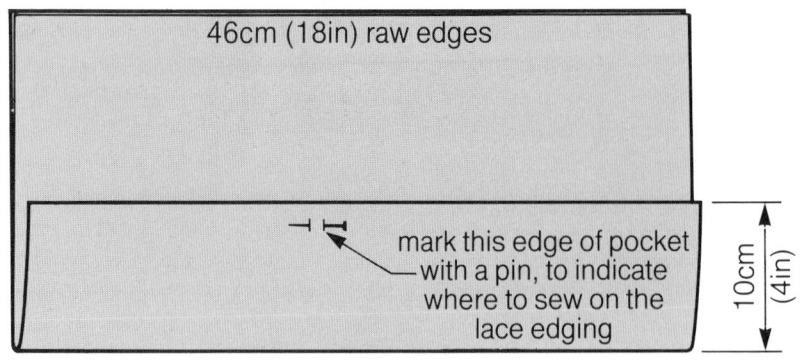

46cm (18in) raw edges

mark this edge of pocket
with a pin, to indicate
where to sew on the
lace edging

10cm
(4in)

DIAGRAM 3
showing how to turn up fabric
to form deepest pockets on skirt

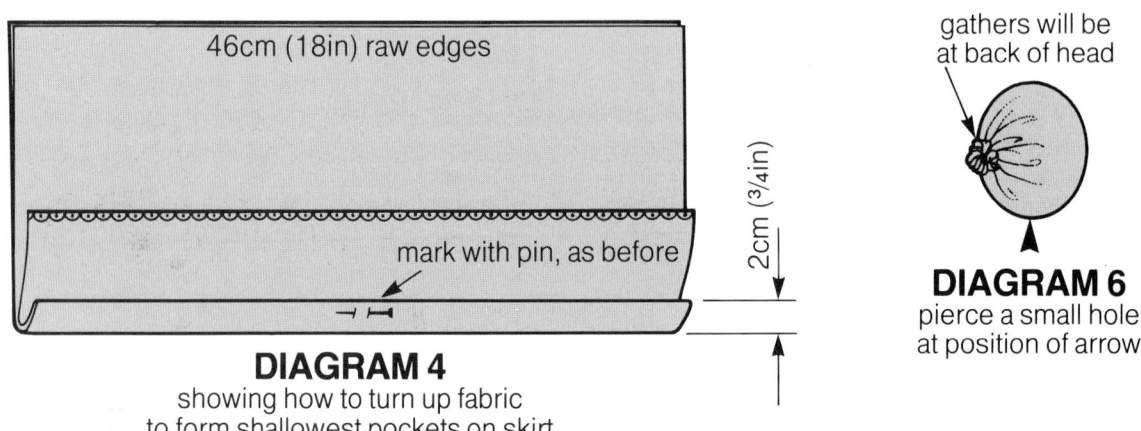

46cm (18in) raw edges

mark with pin, as before

2cm (³/₄in)

DIAGRAM 4
showing how to turn up fabric
to form shallowest pockets on skirt

gathers will be
at back of head

DIAGRAM 6
pierce a small hole
at position of arrow

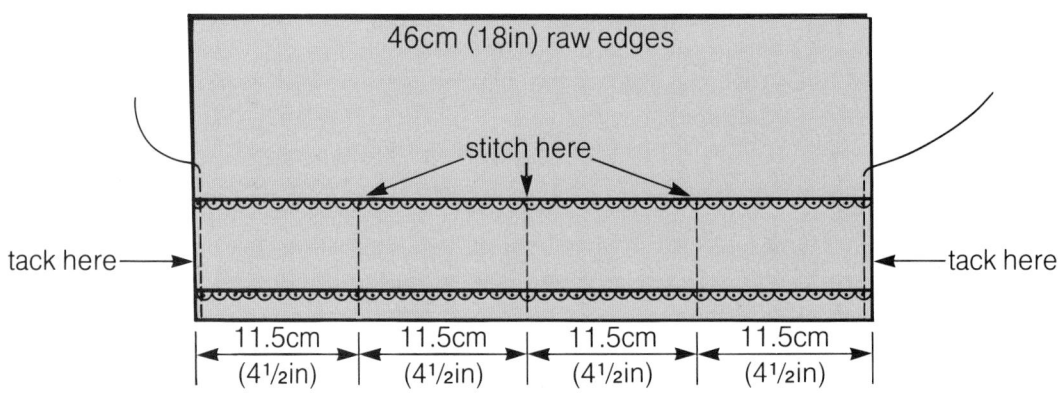

46cm (18in) raw edges

stitch here

tack here →

← tack here

11.5cm
(4¹/₂in)

11.5cm
(4¹/₂in)

11.5cm
(4¹/₂in)

11.5cm
(4¹/₂in)

DIAGRAM 5
showing how to stitch pocket folds to
separate into four pockets

eye-line, taking thread through to face from back of head to do this. Work small stitches for nose and mouth in red thread, as shown in the photograph. Colour cheeks with red pencil. Glue a piece of lace trimming around the cone, below head.

The hair
Wind a strand of yarn ten times around a 16cm (6¼in) long piece of card. Remove from card carefully and sew centres of strands to forehead 2cm (¾in) above the eyes. Take yarn strands to each side of head and sew them to head, level with mouth.

Make two more hair pieces in same way and sew the centres behind the first hair piece, but let these strands hang down the back of the head. Catch them to head, spacing them out evenly.

The shawl
Cut a 20cm (8in) square of plain fabric, to tone with the other fabrics used. Turn in all the raw edges 3mm (⅛in) and stitch down.

Fold the shawl corner to opposite corner, having right side outside and tack all the edges together except for fold. Stitch lace trimming to the tacked edges only. This will be the right side of the shawl.

Place the shawl around the doll's shoulders, turning in folded edge at back of neck as necessary for a neat fit. Gather up front ends of shawl, as shown in the photograph, leaving the points hanging down, then fasten off. Catch the shawl gathers to the skirt with a few stitches. Sew a ribbon bow to gathers.

The bonnet
Cut the bonnet from folded plain fabric, placing edge indicated on pattern to fold. Join curved edges, taking a 3mm (⅛in) seam and leaving a gap in the seam for turning. Turn right side out and press, then slip stitch gap.

Run a gathering thread around, 2cm (¾in) away from the curved edge, as shown on the pattern. Pull up gathers so as to fit across top of head from one side to the other. Fasten off.

Run a second gathering thread along the folded edge, as shown on the pattern. Place bonnet on doll's head, then pull up these gathers to fit across the back of the head and fasten off. Sew a piece of lace trimming to this edge.

Push a little cotton wool inside bonnet to shape it, then sew it to head through all the gathers. Glue a strip of lace trimming over gathers at top of head to match the lace already used on back of bonnet. Add a few gathered ribbon rosettes to top of hat.

SCENTED HATS AND BASKETS

These miniature hats (8cm (3in) across) are easy to make from strips and circles of dress-lining material, trimmed with rosebuds and ribbon.

The baskets are simpler still – they are made from the plastic lids of aerosol cans, covered with pretty fabric and topped with net to hold the pot-pourri in place. You can use any kind of aerosol lid, or even lids off other containers, since the instructions are written to cover all sizes.

For the hats you will need: Oddments of dress-lining or other thin fabric; rosebud or lace trimming; felt; ribbon; lavender flowers.

For the baskets you will need: Lids as described; oddments of printed fabric; net fabric; pot-pourri; ribbon and lace edging or braid; adhesive.

Note: Seams are as stated in the instructions.

To make the hat
For top of hat cut a 9cm (3½in) diameter circle of fabric. Gather around the edge and fill with lavender flowers, then pull up gathers tightly and fasten off.

For hat brim, cut an 8×28cm (3×11in) strip of fabric. Fold fabric, right side outside, bringing the long edges together. Press. Open up fabric and join short ends, taking a 5mm (¼in) seam. Press seam open. Fold strip again, as it was pressed, then gather around the long raw edges. Pull up gathers until the raw edges meet, then fasten off.

Sew top of hat to brim, placing gathers of both together. Sew rosebud or other trimming around top of

hat near to brim, as shown in the colour photograph.

Make a small ribbon bow, leaving long ends on the ribbon. Turn these ends under and catch them underneath bow, forming ribbon loops which can be placed over a coathanger hook. Sew bow to hat, as shown in the photograph. Now sew a small circle of felt, to match fabric, underneath hat to cover the raw edges.

To make the basket

Fill the lid with pot-pourri almost to top. Cut a circle of net, making it about 1cm (⅜in) larger all round than top of lid. Place net over open top of lid and glue edge of circle onto side of lid, pulling net tight as you do this.

Cut a strip of printed fabric, twice the depth of your lid, plus 1cm (⅜in); by the measurement around the circumference of lid plus 1cm (⅜in). Note that if your lid has a wider protruding rim (as in the smaller basket illustrated), the depth measurement should be taken *below* the rim.

Join the ends of the fabric strip, taking a 5mm (³⁄₁₆in) seam. Now fold this tube of fabric in half, right side outside, bringing the long raw edges together. Tack these edges together.

Slip the tube onto the lid and stick the folded top edge level with top of lid, or below the rim. Gather around the tacked raw edges, then spread a little glue around the edge of lid base. Pull up gathers, drawing the raw edges of fabric onto base, then fasten off. Cut a circle of felt slightly smaller than base, then glue it in place to cover raw edges. Glue lace edging or braid around top edge of fabric, or around the rim of the lid.

For the basket handle, cut a 4×14cm (1½×5½in) strip of printed fabric. Turn in the long raw edges 1cm (³⁄₈in) and press. Fold strip in half along length, having right side outside, then press. Stitch through handle at both long edges. Glue ends of handles securely to sides of basket, then add ribbon bows as shown in the photograph.

To vary this design, you could make the baskets (omitting the net covering), then fill them with a few tiny sweets or chocolates wrapped in a twist of Cellophane or clear plastic and tied with a ribbon bow.

DOLLY-PEG DOLLS

Dolls made from the old-fashioned type of wooden clothes-peg are sure to be popular at bazaars and sales of work and they are such fun to make.

Each of the dolls illustrated in the colour photograph has a different purpose. You can make the one on the left with the wide crinoline skirt as a delightful fashionable lady of the Victorian era, and her skirt can also *be used as a pincushion. The centre doll is an egg-cosy and the one on the right is a sachet filled with lavender flowers.*

Each one is about 13cm (5in) high and they are all constructed in the same basic way, except for the skirts. I used plain shiny dress-lining fabric for the dresses and decorated them with ribbon frills and rosebud trimming.

PATCHWORK QUILT

Although this quilt looks as though it took years to complete, it is relatively quick and easy to make. It is composed of an arrangement of 20cm (about 8in) squares, joined diagonally, so that the finished quilt has a chevron edge.

Each of the squares is made up from either four small squares, or two triangles of fabric sewn together. Each square is padded and lined separately, then they are all machine-stitched together. The chevron points are decorated with pretty fabric tassels filled with wadding.

You will need five different patterned fabrics for the quilt, which is designed to fit a standard double bed. All quantities given are for 91cm (36in) wide fabrics. Make sure all the fabrics used are washable.

You will need (see Diagram 6):
5m (5½yd) of fabric A (dark green)
1.50m (1¾yd) of fabric B (green patterned)
1m (1⅛yd) of fabric C (pink gingham)
1.70m (2yd) of fabric D (green gingham)
3m (3⅜yd) of fabric E (pink patterned)
6m (6⅝yd) of plain fabric for lining
8m (9yd) of polyester wadding
Thin card and adhesive for making the templates.

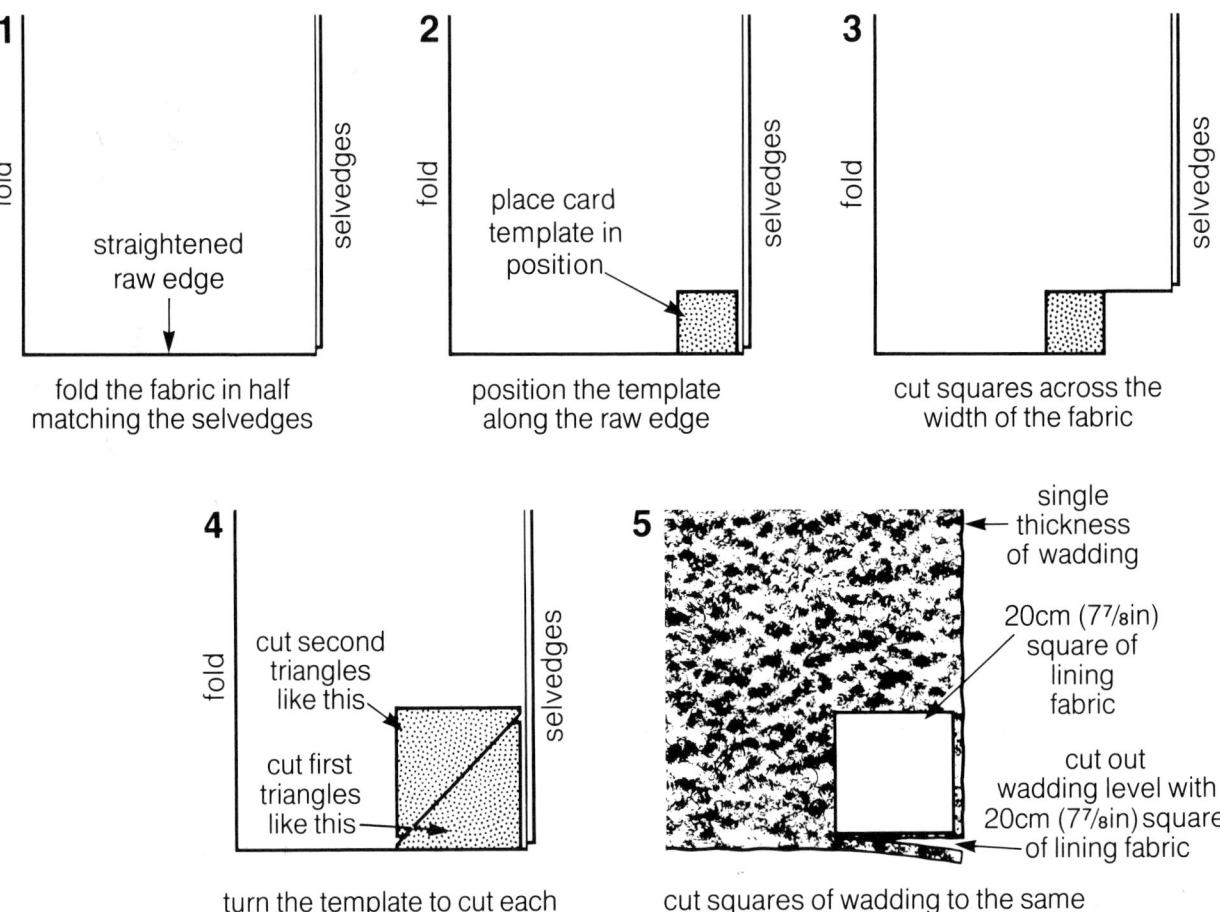

1 fold the fabric in half matching the selvedges

fold — straightened raw edge — selvedges

2 position the template along the raw edge

fold — place card template in position — selvedges

3 cut squares across the width of the fabric

fold — selvedges

4 turn the template to cut each alternate patch

fold — cut second triangles like this — cut first triangles like this — selvedges

5 cut squares of wadding to the same size as the lining squares

single thickness of wadding
20cm (7⅞in) square of lining fabric
cut out wadding level with 20cm (7⅞in) square of lining fabric

Notes: Read through all the preliminary instructions before starting to make any of the patches, and make all the patches before joining any of them together.

Seams measuring 1cm (⅜in) are allowed on all pieces unless otherwise stated. Cut all the squares and triangles on the straight grain of the fabric, as shown in the diagrams. Join all pieces with right sides together.

When making each patch, press all patchwork seams open as the work progresses. Lightly press the finished patches with a steam iron. As you join the patches to each other, lightly steam-press the seams, first on the wrong side, then on the right side of the work.

To make the templates
Only two shapes are required – a square and a triangle,

both of which can be traced off the page. The triangle has been *halved* to fit the page, so trace it onto folded paper, placing the fold to the edge indicated, then cut it out with the paper folded. Refer to p. 11 to see how to do this accurately. Open up the paper and the piece will now look like the small diagram shown alongside the template.

Glue the square and triangular paper shapes onto thin card, then cut out the card level with the edges of the paper shapes.

Method of cutting out patchwork pieces
Because the squares and triangles are cut from various fabrics, it is best to cut them out for *each* round of the quilt in turn as they are needed, by referring to

6-guide to patterned fabrics

fabric A
(dark green)

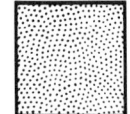
fabric B
(green patterned)

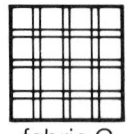
fabric C
(pink gingham)

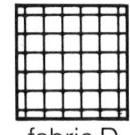
fabric D
(green gingham)

fabric E
(pink patterned)

7-make the required number of patches as shown below

centre
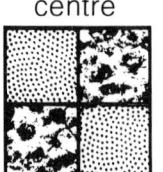
make 2
(using A & B)

1st round
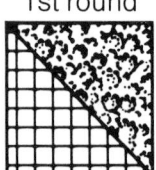
make 8
(using D & E)

2nd round

make 12
(using A & C)

3rd round
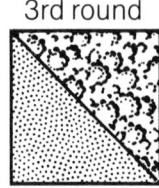
make 16
(using B & E)

4th round

make 20
(using A & D)

5th round

make 24
(using A, C & E)

6th round
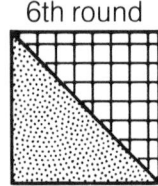
make 28
(using B & D)

7th round

make 32
(using A & E)

8-Arrange
the patches then
join in rows,
following the
direction of the
arrows

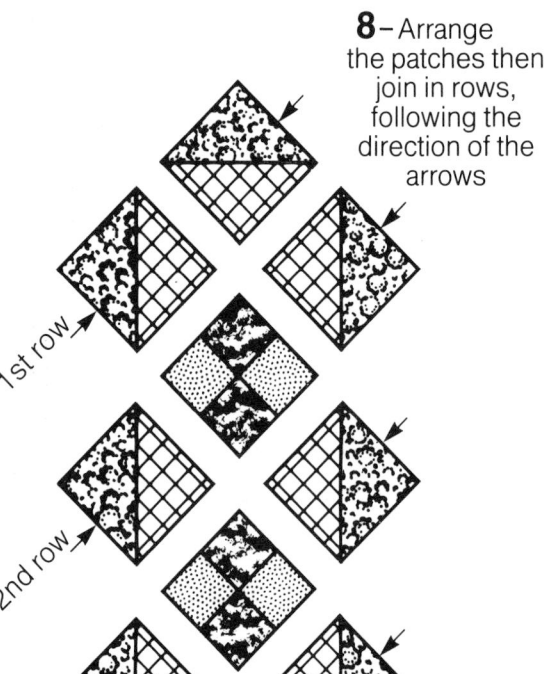

1st row
2nd row
3rd row
4th row

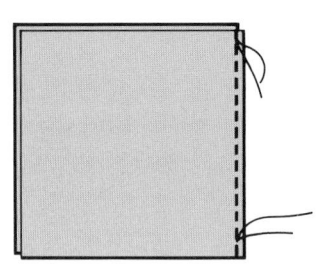

9-Machine
the patches
together, right
sides facing,
taking a tiny
seam, and backstitching
at each end of seam

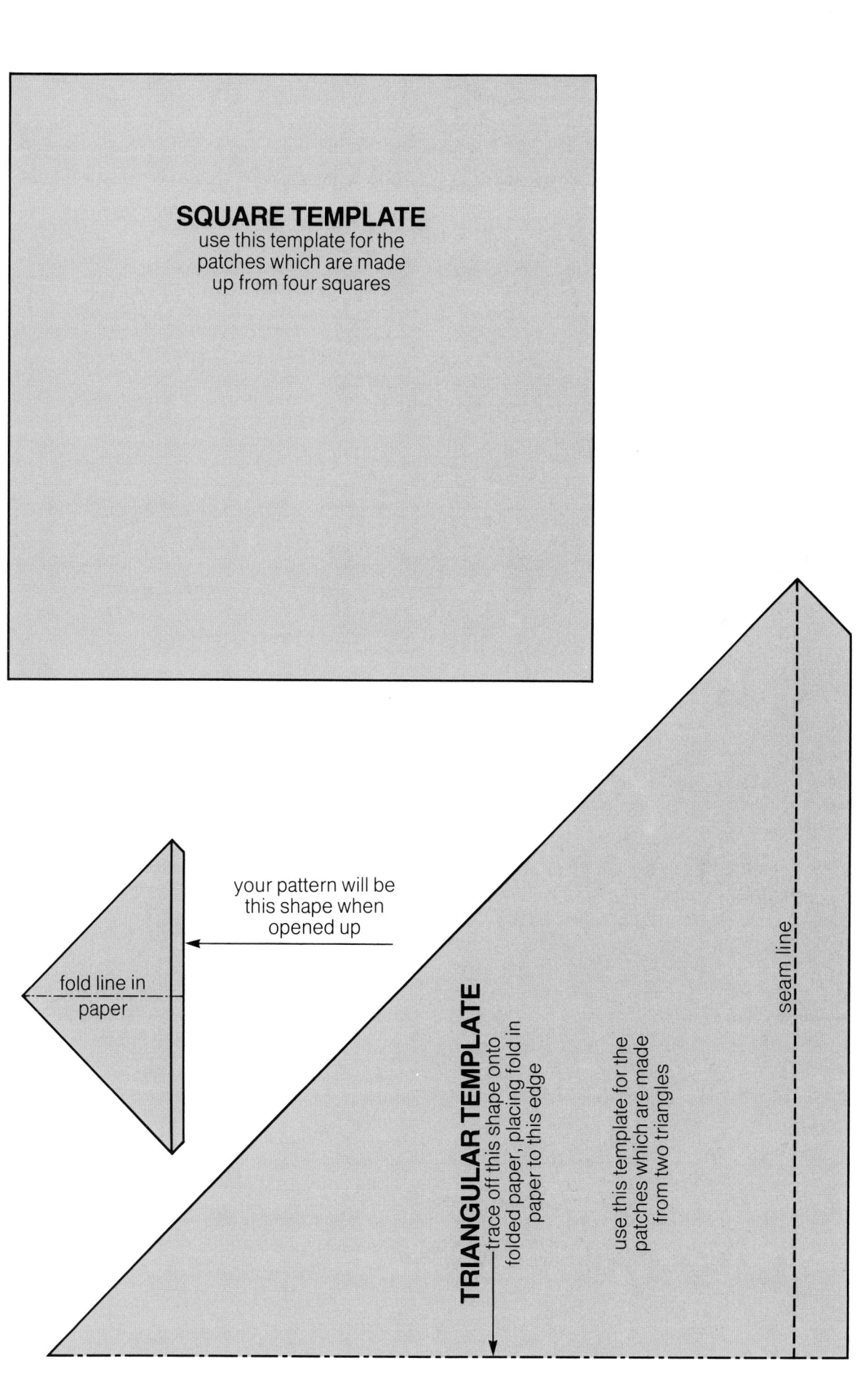

SQUARE TEMPLATE
use this template for the
patches which are made
up from four squares

your pattern will be
this shape when
opened up

fold line in
paper

TRIANGULAR TEMPLATE
trace off this shape onto
folded paper, placing fold in
paper to this edge

use this template for the
patches which are made
from two triangles

seam line

Diagram 7. The following instructions are given only as a guide to the most economical method of cutting out the pieces.

First straighten one raw edge of the piece of fabric by pulling a thread across the width, then trimming along this line.

Fold the fabric in half, wrong side out, bringing the selvedges together as shown in Diagram 1. To cut out the square patches, place the template on the fabric just within the selvedges, with one edge of square level with straightened raw edges, as shown in Diagram 2. Draw around the edges of the template, then pin the two layers of fabric together and cut out the squares. Repeat this across the width of the fabric, as shown in Diagram 3. You will now have been able to cut eight fabric squares altogether, from the width of the fabric.

For the triangular patches, straighten and fold the fabric as before, then place the template in the position shown in Diagram 4, draw around it and cut out in the same way as for squares. To cut the next two triangles, turn the template as shown in Diagram 4. A total of eight fabric triangles can be cut across the width if you do this.

To cut the lining pieces

Make a 20cm (7⅞in) square template as for the other templates. Cut out the lining pieces by drawing around the template in the same way as for the other pieces. You will need 110 squares of lining fabric. Using the same template, cut 32 squares from fabric A. These are used for lining the *outer* 32 patches on the quilt only.

To ensure that you take exactly straight 1cm (⅜in) seams when making up the patchwork squares, make an 18cm (7⅛in) square template as for the other templates.

After cutting out each lining square, place the 18cm (7⅛in) template centrally on the wrong side of the lining square and draw a line around it with a pencil, to mark the seam line.

To cut the wadding squares

Use one of the 20cm (7⅞in) lining squares for a pattern. Place this on a single layer of wadding, then cut the wadding level with the edges of the lining square, as shown in Diagram 5. You will need 142 squares of wadding.

To cut out the required number of patches

Diagram 6 gives a guide to the different patterned fabrics. Following this, cut out the squares and triangles from each fabric as necessary, to make the number of finished patches for each round, as indicated in Diagram 7. For example, for the centre of the quilt you need 4 squares of fabric A and 4 of fabric B, to make the required 2 patches. For the 1st round of patches, you need 8 triangles of fabric D and 8 of fabric E, to make the required 8 patches.

To join the patchwork pieces

Join the small square patches in pairs at one edge. Now join the pairs together to make a square, taking care that they are arranged using the various patterned fabrics, as shown in Diagram 7 for each round.

Join the triangular pieces together along the diagonal edges.

To make up the patched squares

Place each finished patched square right side up, on top of a wadding square, then place a lining piece wrong side up on top of the patch. Note when making up the outermost round of patches that you should use the 32 lining squares which were cut from fabric A.

Pin the pieces together at the corners, having all the raw edges level. Machine around the edges through all the thicknesses, following the pencilled seam line, and leaving a small gap in one edge for turning. Trim the seam at each corner, then turn the patch right side out, using a knitting-needle to ease out the corners. Turn in the raw edges of the gap and slip stitch.

To make up the quilt

First lay out the centre 2 patches and arrange the 1st round of 8 patches around these as shown in Diagram 8. Join the 2 patches in the 1st row (see Diagram 8), as follows. Place them right sides together and pin. Machine-stitch along the edges to be joined through all thicknesses, taking a tiny seam as shown in Diagram 9 and working machine back stitching at each end of the seam to secure.

Now join the 2nd, 3rd and 4th rows in the same way, as indicated in Diagram 8. Join the rows to each other at the edges where they touch, to keep the arrangement shown in the diagram.

Arrange the next 12 patches around this piece, the next 16 around these and the next 20 around these. Join the pieces in rows as before, then sew them to the centre of the quilt as arranged. Continue in this way until all the patches have been joined.

To make the tassels (makes 32)

For each tassel, cut two 7×12cm (2¾×4¾in) pieces using fabric E. Join the pieces around the edges, leaving open at one short end. Trim the seam at the corners and turn the tassel right side out. Stuff the tassel with teased out bits of wadding, then run a gathering thread around, 1cm (⅜in) away from the raw edge. Pull up gathers tightly, turning the raw edge to the inside, then fasten off, leaving enough length of thread for sewing the tassel to the quilt.

Tie a length of double sewing thread tightly around the tassel, 3.5cm (1⅜in) away from the gathered top. Sew the thread ends into the tassel. Sew a tassel to each outer point of the quilt.

COSY SNOWMAN

This frosty snowman is really quite hot stuff, because his tubby body forms a hand-muff, guaranteed to keep tiny fingers warm in the coldest of weather!

His striped bobble cap and removable scarf are knitted from oddments of yarn and the scarf is simple enough for a child to knit. There is also a small buttoned purse sewn on the back of the snowman for holding little treasures, or pocket money and a handkerchief. The snowman measures 35cm (14in) from top to toe.

You will need: 30cm (⅜yd) of 138cm (54in) wide white fur fabric; small piece of black fabric for feet and purse; two domed black buttons about 1.5cm (⅝in) in diameter for the eyes; a 1cm (⅜in) diameter orange button for the nose; small button for purse fastening; 70cm (¾yd) of strong braid for neck strap; a little stuffing; red thread; oddments of double knitting yarn (USA: worsted weight); a pair of 3¾mm, (No 9, USA: 4) knitting-needles.

Notes: All patterns can be traced off the page. The body, head, foot and hand patterns should be traced onto folded paper, placing the folded edge to the dotted line indicated on each pattern. Cut them out folded, then open up to give the complete pattern. Mark matching details onto each half of body and head patterns.

Take care to have the smooth stroke of the fur pile in the direction shown on each pattern, when cutting out. Take 1cm (⅜in) seams on all pieces, unless otherwise stated.

The body

Cut out pieces as they are mentioned so as to follow any special instructions for each piece.

Cut one body piece from fur fabric for the front of body, and, before removing pattern, mark position of hands and feet at edges of fabric with pencil.

Cut four foot pieces from black fabric and join them in pairs, leaving the lower edges open. Trim seams, turn right side out and press. Tack the lower edges of feet to marked positions, on right side of fabric, having

the raw edges level and feet pointing inwards. Pin the curved edges of feet to fur fabric to keep them out of the way.

Cut four hand pieces from fur fabric and join them in pairs, leaving lower edges open. Turn right side out. Tack lower edges to sides of body in same way as for feet. Pin them to body to keep them out of the way.

Now cut two purse pieces from black fabric. Join them around the edges, leaving a gap in one edge for turning. Trim the seam at the corners, then turn right side out and press. If your machine makes buttonholes, make one at the position shown. If not, stitch at lines shown, then cut fabric open between stitching and oversew around the raw edges.

Cut another body piece for the back and, before removing the pattern, mark corner positions of pocket

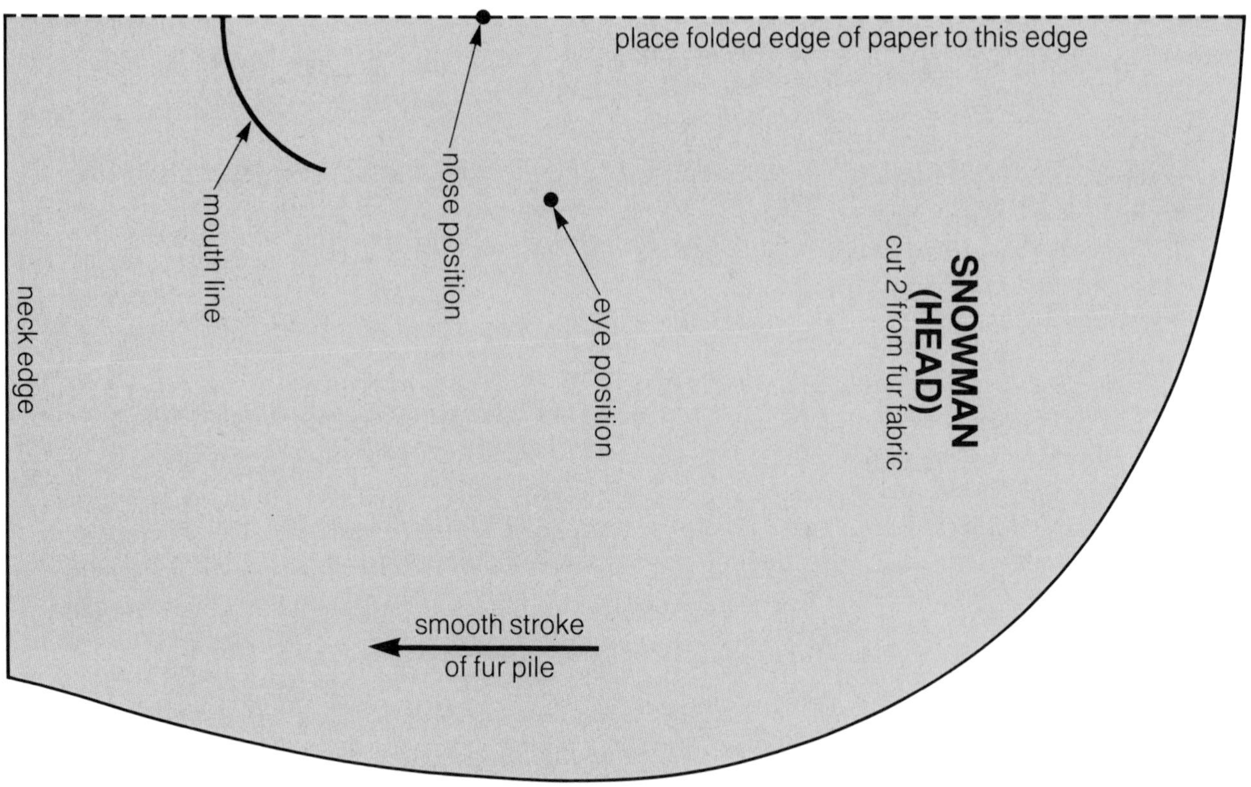

place folded edge of paper to this edge

mouth line

nose position

eye position

neck edge

**SNOWMAN
(HEAD)**
cut 2 from fur fabric

smooth stroke
of fur pile

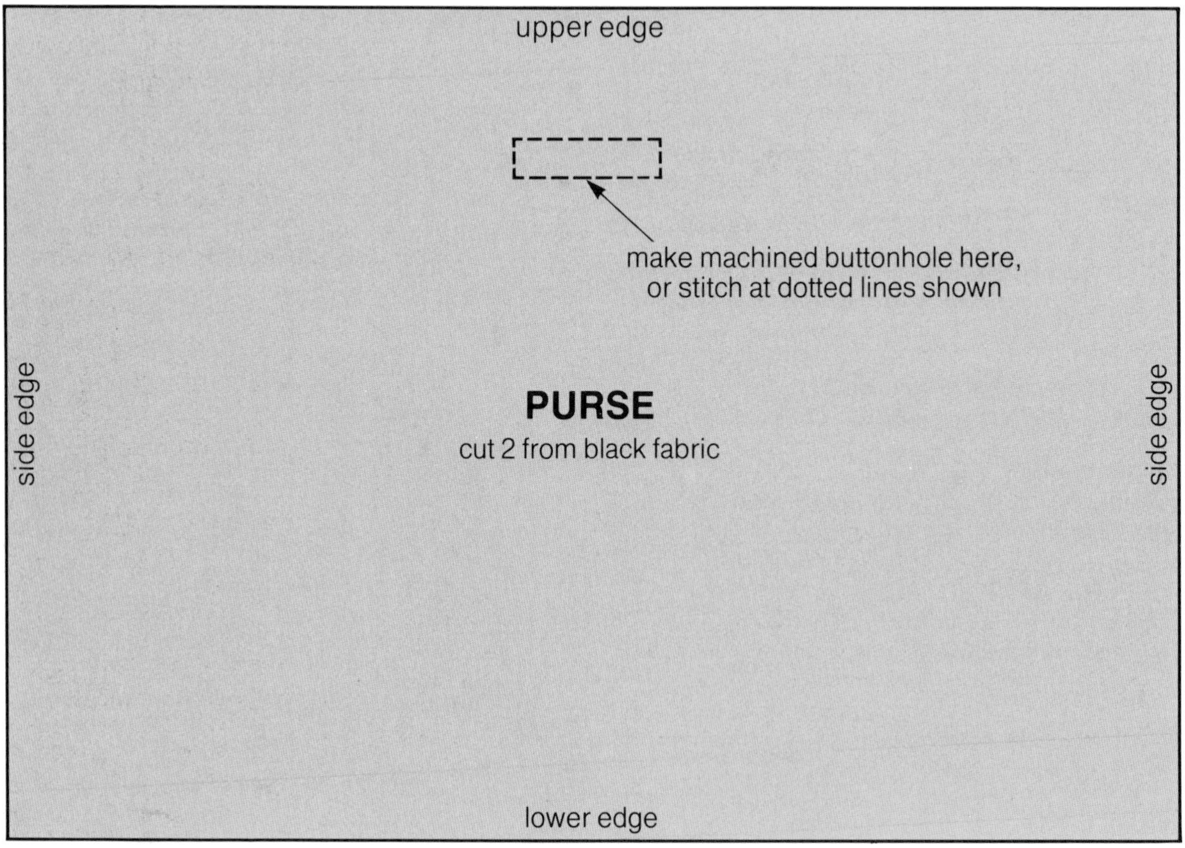

upper edge

make machined buttonhole here,
or stitch at dotted lines shown

side edge

PURSE
cut 2 from black fabric

side edge

lower edge

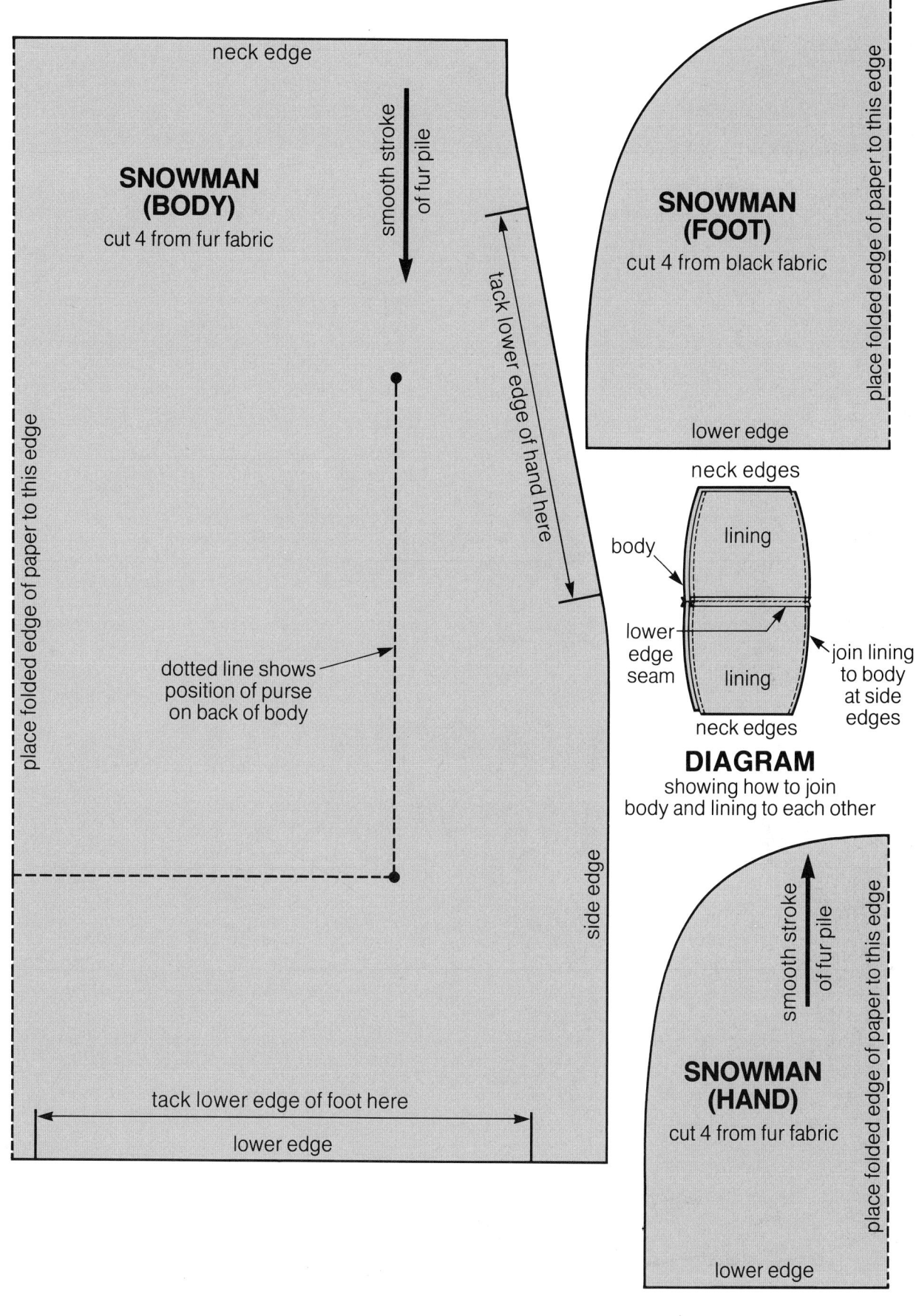

SNOWMAN (BODY)

cut 4 from fur fabric

neck edge

smooth stroke of fur pile

place folded edge of paper to this edge

tack lower edge of hand here

dotted line shows position of purse on back of body

side edge

tack lower edge of foot here

lower edge

SNOWMAN (FOOT)

cut 4 from black fabric

place folded edge of paper to this edge

lower edge

neck edges

body

lining

lower edge seam

lining

join lining to body at side edges

neck edges

DIAGRAM

showing how to join body and lining to each other

SNOWMAN (HAND)

cut 4 from fur fabric

smooth stroke of fur pile

place folded edge of paper to this edge

lower edge

with pencil point, right through to right side of fabric. Stitch side and lower edges of purse in position on right side. Join this body piece to front body at lower edges, then trim seam.

For the muff lining, cut two more body pieces and join them at the lower edges, then trim seam. Place the body and lining pieces right sides together, as shown in the diagram, having all the raw edges of both level. Join them to each other all down the side edges. Turn right side out through one open neck edge. Remove pins from hands and feet.

Bring all the raw neck edges together, having the lining on the inside to form the muff, then oversew all the neck edges together. Turn feet up onto the front of body and slip stitch edges in place.

The head

Cut two head pieces from fur fabric and, before removing pattern from second piece, mark position of nose and eyes by pushing pencil point through pattern and into fabric. Mark mouth line with dots at intervals also, then remove pattern and join up the dots. Having wrong side of fabric uppermost, machine-stitch several times along the mouth line using red thread. Draw thread ends through to wrong side of fabric and knot.

Sew buttons for eyes and nose to marked positions on right side of fabric. Join head pieces to each other, leaving neck edges open. Turn right side out and stuff lightly, keeping head fairly flat.

Now push neck edges of body 1cm (⅜in) inside open neck edges of head. Slip stitch neck edges of head to body.

The scarf

Cast on 8 stitches and work in garter stitch (every row knit) until scarf measures 56cm (22in). Cast off. Add yarn fringe to each end of the scarf, then tie it around snowman's neck.

The cap

Cast on 80 stitches and work 6 rows in single rib. Change to stocking stitch (knit 1 row, purl 1 row alternately) and work 18 rows in two-row stripes in colours of your choice. Keeping the sequence of stripes correct, shape top of cap. 1st row: knit 2 stitches together, all across row. 2nd row: purl. Repeat these 2 rows twice more. Break off yarn, leaving a long end. Thread it through the remaining 10 stitches, pull up tightly and fasten off. Join row ends. Make a pom-pom and sew it to top of cap.

Place cap on snowman's head at a jaunty angle, as shown in the colour photograph, having cap seam at centre back. Sew to head through first row of rib.

Pin the ends of the braid (for neck strap) to back of snowman's head, 6cm (2¼in) up from neck and 10cm (4in) apart. Adjust length of braid if necessary to fit child, then sew ends in place.

A QUARTET OF CUSHIONS

Here are some ideas for making cushions with an authentic touch of Victoriana. You may have the odd length of hand-made lace trimming from an old tray cloth or pillow-case which is too small or fragile to sew on a garment, but which can be displayed quite beautifully in a cushion.

There seems to be a profusion of crocheted lace mats from the past and I used one of these for the central cushion, mounted on a piece of velvet. The square cushion is made from machine-stitched fabric strips and the hexagonal cushion from small patches, sewn in the traditional way by hand.

When making the cushions, I was using a cloth for pressing which had been washed so often that the rose pattern had faded to delicate pale shades. This eventually ended up in the fourth cushion, together with a length of lace trimming and two butterflies which I had saved for many years.

Avoid using pure white if you want

an antique effect and choose cotton fabrics with subdued colours. The rectangular cushion measures 28 × 38cm (11 × 15in) and the hexagonal cushion is 42cm (16½in) across the centre from point to point. Each cushion is filled with a pad made from polyester wadding.

You will need: Velvet, printed fabrics and lace trimmings, ribbon and lace mats, as suggested; polyester wadding for filling the cushions; thin card for patchwork templates; thin paper; a craft knife; adhesive.

Notes: Patterns are given full-size for the hexagonal patchwork templates. Seams are as stated in the instructions. Complete details are given for making the patchwork cushions, but for the others only outline instructions are given because these depend on the availability of materials.

GENERAL INSTRUCTIONS
(for all the cushions)

To appliqué shapes on to fabric

Place a wooden board or piece of thick card under the cushion fabric. Having the right side of fabric uppermost, pin the shapes to be appliquéd at intervals all around the edges, pushing pins at right angles through the fabric or lace and into the board or card.

Slip stitch all around the edges of the shapes, using matching sewing thread and small stitches, and removing the pins as you go. This is the easiest way of sewing pieces to velvet in particular, because the pile tends to move the pieces about.

To make up the cushions

Cut a piece of backing fabric the same size as the cushion front. Join the pieces, taking a 1cm (⅜in) seam unless otherwise stated, leaving a large opening in one edge. Turn right side out and insert the cushion pad, then turn in the raw edges of gap and slip stitch neatly.

To make the cushion pads

Cut out four pieces of wadding the same size as the *finished* cushion-cover. Now cut out another piece of wadding about 4cm (1½in) smaller all round than the first shapes. Cut another about 8cm (3in) smaller all round than the first shapes.

Place the smaller shapes centrally between the layers of the larger shapes, then oversew all the outer edges of the largest shapes together.

STRIP PATCHWORK CUSHION

You will need seven different patterned fabrics, all 91cm (36in) in width. Tear or cut a 4cm (1½in) wide strip from each fabric across the full 91cm (36in) width.

Now join the fabric strips at the long edges, taking 5mm (¼in) seams and pressing all the seams open as you go. Your piece of patchwork will now measure 22cm (7½in) in width×91cm (36in) long. Cut four 22cm (7½in) long pieces from the length of the piece and discard the remaining oddment.

Arrange the squares as shown in the photograph. Join two pairs of adjacent squares, then join the pairs, taking 5mm (¼in) seams, pressing the seams open as before. Cut a strip of lace trimming to fit around the outer edge of the patchwork, plus a bit extra for joining the ends and easing at the corners. Join the ends. Tack the straight edge of lace around the edges of patchwork on right side, having the fancy edge of lace pointing inwards and gathering lace slightly at corners of fabric.

Now make up the cushion as given in the general instructions, taking a 5mm (¼in) seam when sewing on the backing fabric.

BUTTERFLIES AND ROSES

For the basic cushion I used a 30×40cm (11¾×15¾in) piece of red velvet and a matching piece for the backing.

Cut four 5cm (2in) wide strips of striped fabric for the frame around the central motifs, or whatever width suits the striped fabric you are using.

Arrange the strips on the cushion piece and cut them at each corner to mitre as in a picture frame. Turn in all the raw edges of fabric about 5mm (¼in) and tack.

Appliqué the fabric pieces to the cushion fabric, sewing all the edges in place, as given in the general instructions. Pin lace trimming around the outer edge of the frame, gathering it slightly at each corner. Sew both long edges of the trimming in place.

Cut and sew on patches of fabric for the central motifs, or whatever you wish to use. Make up the cushion as described in the general instructions.

LACE MAT CUSHION

Cut the cushion fabric piece about 4cm (1½in) larger all round than the lace mat.

Appliqué the mat to the fabric around the edges, as described in general instructions. Continue catching

the mat to fabric with rows of small straight stitches, working towards the centre. Make up the cushion as given in the general instructions.

HEXAGONAL CUSHION

Trace the two patterns off the page, marking the dotted line on the larger pattern. Cut them out and glue them onto card. Use a craft knife to cut out the centre of the

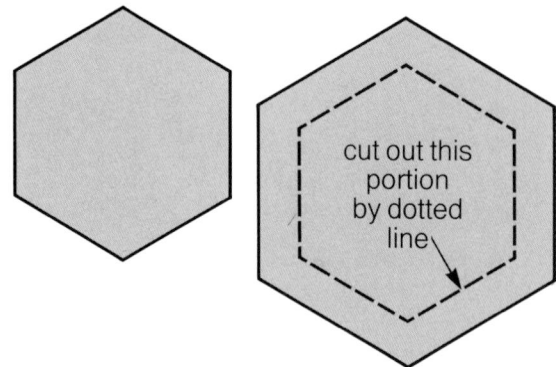

cut out this portion by dotted line

larger template at the dotted line shown. This forms a window through which the fabric pattern can be seen if you want to pick a particular motif when cutting out the patches. Now cut both templates from the card, level with the paper shapes.

Choose pieces of fabric for the patchwork pieces and decide how they will be arranged. I used four different fabrics, starting with a single flower picked out of one patterned fabric for the central patch and introducing the same patches at intervals, as shown in the photograph. If you wish to use the same arrangement, you will need a total of 61 fabric patches as follows: single flower, 13; mauve-patterned, 12; red-patterned, 18; flower-printed, 18.

Alternatively, if you have plenty of fabric, you can cut rough trial patches from various prints and keep moving them around until you have a pleasing arrangement.

To make the patches

Draw around the edges of the largest template onto the fabric and cut out as many patches as required. If you wish to pick out a single flower or other motif on a patch, use the window to position the template before drawing around it.

Place the smaller template onto three or four layers of thin paper, then hold the template and paper pieces securely together with one hand and cut out paper patches level with the edges of card.

Pin a paper patch centrally on the wrong side of a fabric patch. Fold each raw edge of the patch in turn over the edge of the paper shape and tack as you go through the fabric and paper.

When all the patches are completed, arrange them as

required on a table. Take the centre patch and an adjacent one and place them right sides together with all edges level. Join them along one straight edge, using a thin needle and small oversewing stitches.

Now add patches one at a time in the same way, oversewing them together at their adjacent edges. When the piece is completed, press it on wrong side with a warm iron over a damp cloth. Remove all the tacking threads, then press again on the right side. Remove paper shapes.

To make the cushion-cover
Cut a hexagon of fabric about 8cm (3in) larger all

round than the patchwork piece. Sew patchwork to fabric around the edges, as described in the general instructions.

Cut a length of lace trimming about 6cm (2¼in) in width, to fit around the hexagon about 2cm (¾in) away from the edges of patchwork, adding a little extra for pleating at the corners. Tack, then hand-sew lace in place, making small inverted pleats at each corner and joining the ends of lace at one corner also.

Sew a small ribbon bow to each pleated corner. Make up the cushion as given in the general instructions, taking care not to catch the lace in the seam.

VELVET FRAMED PICTURES

It's so easy to turn a pretty postcard or greetings card into an attractive framed picture – no carpentry required, just scraps of velvet, card and trimmings.

I chose a couple of matching postcard prints, depicting plants and wild life and the completed pictures are just a bit larger than the original postcards.

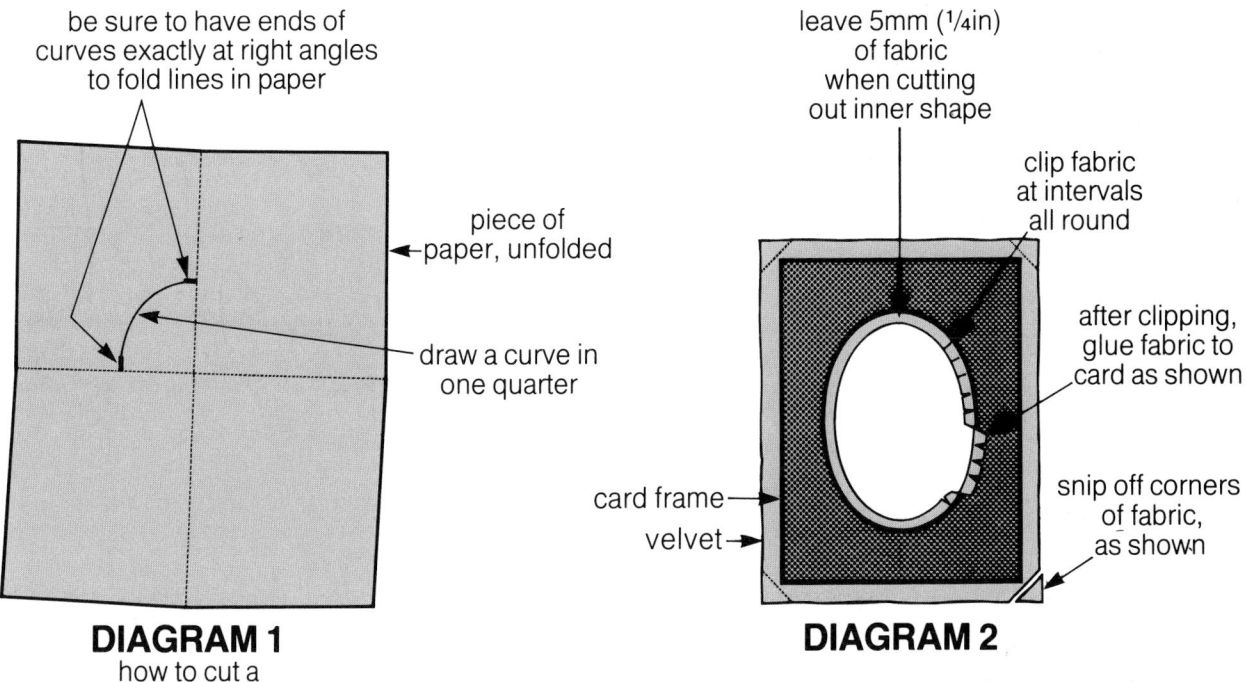

be sure to have ends of curves exactly at right angles to fold lines in paper

piece of paper, unfolded

draw a curve in one quarter

DIAGRAM 1
how to cut a perfect oval

leave 5mm (¼in) of fabric when cutting out inner shape

clip fabric at intervals all round

after clipping, glue fabric to card as shown

snip off corners of fabric, as shown

card frame

velvet

DIAGRAM 2

You will need: Pictures for framing as suggested, thin strong card; small piece of velvet; narrow gold braid (optional); thin gold cord; adhesive.

Note: The diagrams show how to make the pictures illustrated, but the method is exactly the same whatever shape you make the frame.

To make

First choose your picture, then decide whether you want it to have an oval, rectangular or circular shape surrounding it. You can try the effect with a piece of paper, cutting the required shape from the centre of the paper and adjusting the size according to how much of the picture you wish to be seen.

To cut an oval shape, first fold a piece of paper into quarters, creasing the folds sharply, then open it up again. Draw a curve on one quarter as shown in Diagram 1, estimating roughly the size you will require. Refold the paper and cut along the marked line. When the paper is unfolded, you should have a perfect oval shape. A circular or square opening can be drawn with compasses and ruler.

Now draw a line around the cut-out shape to mark the size of the completed frame. If this shape is to be oval also, then fold and mark the paper as before.

Cut a piece of card the same size as this outer shape. Place the paper on the card and draw around the inner cut-out shape. Cut this marked shape out of the card.

Place the card on the wrong side of a piece of velvet, holding it to the velvet with a few spots of glue. Cut out the velvet 1cm (⅜in) larger all round than the outer edge of the card. Cut out the velvet at the centre of the shape, leaving about 5mm (¼in) of fabric, as shown in Diagram 2.

If your opening is oval or circular, snip this 5mm (¼in) extra fabric at intervals almost to the card, as shown in Diagram 2. If your opening is square or rectangular, snip to the corners only. Turn and glue this extra fabric to the other side of the card. The outer edges will be turned and glued later.

Now glue your postcard or picture on the wrong side of the card so that the desired portion shows through the cut-out shape. Cut another piece of card the same size as the velvet-covered card and glue it to the back of the picture.

Trim off the velvet at each corner as shown in Diagram 2 if your frame is square or rectangular. If it is circular, snip the velvet at intervals almost to the card. Turn all the edges of velvet to the other side of the card and glue down.

Cut another piece of card a bit smaller than the frame, then glue it to the back, enclosing a loop of gold cord at the top for hanging.

You can leave your frame plain or glue on gold braid as shown in the colour photograph.

JUNIOR COATHANGERS

These cute coathangers should encourage children to put their coats away tidily after school. The heads are made from felt, with fur fabric hair that can be brushed for extra play value. A wooden child-sized coathanger is used as a basis for this design.

You will need: A child's wooden coathanger (or you can saw bits off the ends of an adult hanger so that it measures 32cm (12½in) along the curve); small pieces of flesh-coloured felt and brown fur fabric; stuffing; scraps of the following: brown and black felt, polyester wadding, printed cotton fabric, ribbon and lace trimming; a wire coathanger (to provide wire for making the hook at top of head); pliers for cutting and bending wire; red pencil; adhesive; red and white thread.

Notes: Trace the head pattern off the page all around the outline. Mark on the mouth and nose lines. For the *back* hair piece, trace the head pattern as before, but follow the lower dotted hair line shown on the pattern. Trace off *front* hair piece in same way, following the upper dotted hair line. Seams are as stated in the instructions.

To make

First, unscrew the hook which is already on the coathanger and discard it. If the hook is fixed in any other way, snip it off close the wood.

To pad the hanger, cut a piece of wadding the length of the hanger and wide enough to go around the wood, plus 1cm (⅜in) extra on all the edges. Fold the wadding strip over the hanger and oversew all the edges together, enclosing the hanger completely.

To cover the wadding, cut a 10×60cm (4×24in) strip of fabric. Turn in the long raw edges and press, then fold the strip in half along the length, right side out, and press. Run a gathering thread along the centre pressed line of strip, but do not pull up gathers.

Bring the long edges of strip together, having wrong side outside and stitch across the short ends, rounding off the corners. Turn right side out.

Pin the long edges of fabric together, enclosing the hanger at centre. Run a gathering thread through both long edges of the fabric. Pull up these gathers and also the previous gathering thread until the strip fits the hanger. Fasten off the gathering threads.

Before cutting out the head pieces, test your piece of flesh-coloured felt by pulling gently widthways then lengthways, to find the direction in which it stretches most. Cut out two head pieces with most stretch going across head, as shown on the pattern. Mark the mouth and nose lines on one piece only and embroider them in red thread.

Cut one back and one front hair piece from fur fabric, having the smooth stroke of fur pile in direction of arrow on pattern. Lay the hair pieces in position over the head pieces, as shown on pattern, then sew them in place around the edges.

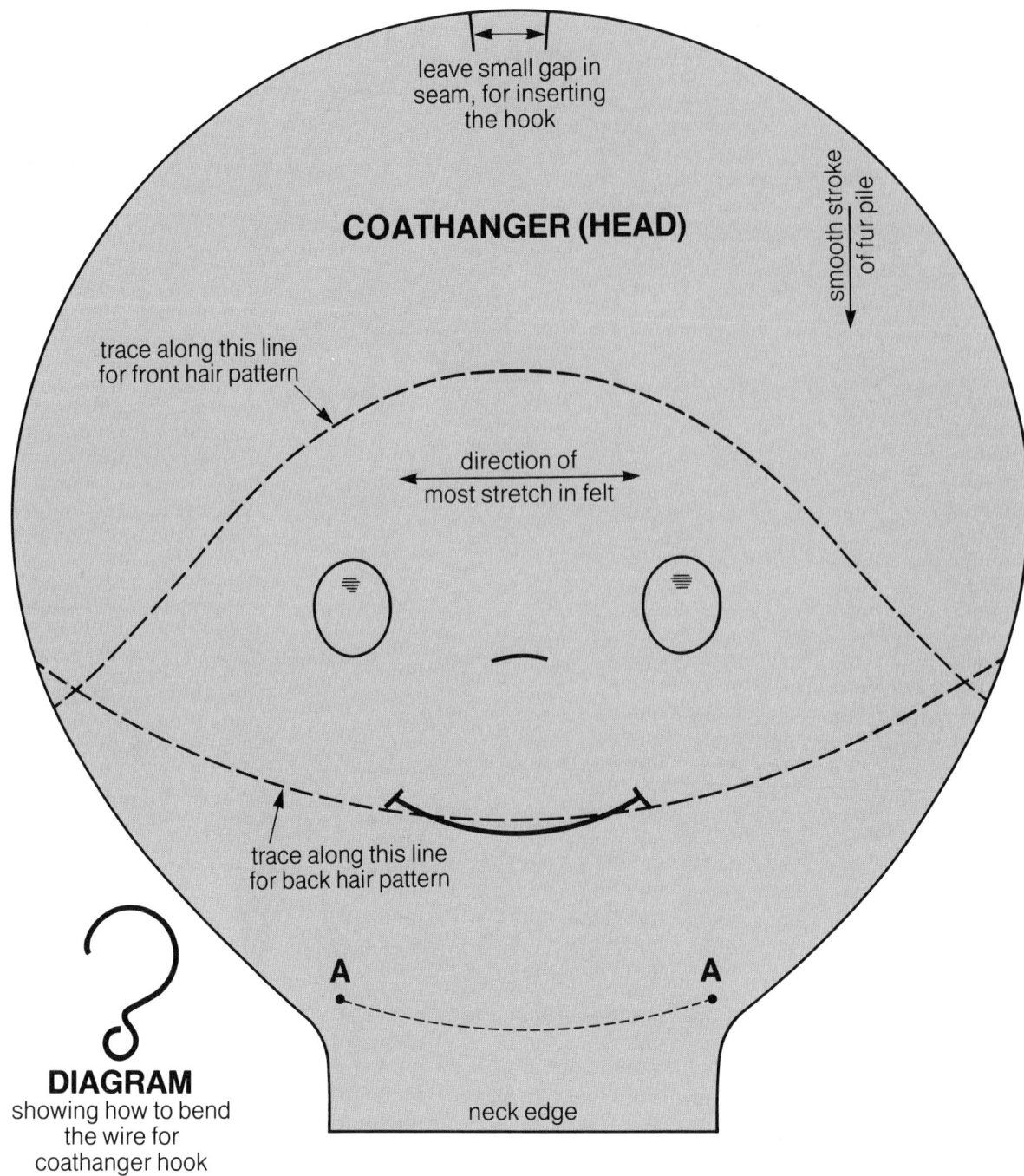

COATHANGER (HEAD)

leave small gap in seam, for inserting the hook

smooth stroke of fur pile

trace along this line for front hair pattern

direction of most stretch in felt

trace along this line for back hair pattern

A   A

DIAGRAM
showing how to bend the wire for coathanger hook

neck edge

Place the head pieces right sides together, sandwiching the hair pieces between them. Join them around the edges, taking a 5mm (¼in) seam, leaving edges open below points A and also leaving a tiny gap in seam at top of head, as shown. Turn head right side out through neck edges and stuff firmly.

Cut the eyes from black felt to size shown on head pattern. Use white thread to work a few stitches on each one, for a highlight. Glue eyes in place. Colour cheeks with red pencil.

Place the open neck edges over the centre of the hanger and sew felt to the hanger fabric along the dotted line A to A at the front, then at the back. Sew the remaining neck edges of felt to hanger.

For the hook, cut a 16cm (6¼in) length off the wire coathanger. Bend one end into a hook shape using pliers, then bend about 3cm (1¼in) of wire at the other end into a circle, as shown in the diagram. Push this circle inside the gap at top of head, then oversew the gap to hold wire securely in place.

Cut a 1.5cm (⅝in) wide strip of brown felt for covering the hook. Oversew the long edges together, enclosing the wire as you go. Catch the end of the felt strip to the head where wire is inserted into head.

For the girl coathanger, gather a length of lace trimming around the neck, joining ends at back. Sew a ribbon bow at the top of the head in front of hook.

For the boy, gather trimming around neck, having ends at centre front for a collar. Sew ribbon bow to front of collar.

CHRISTMAS STOCKINGS

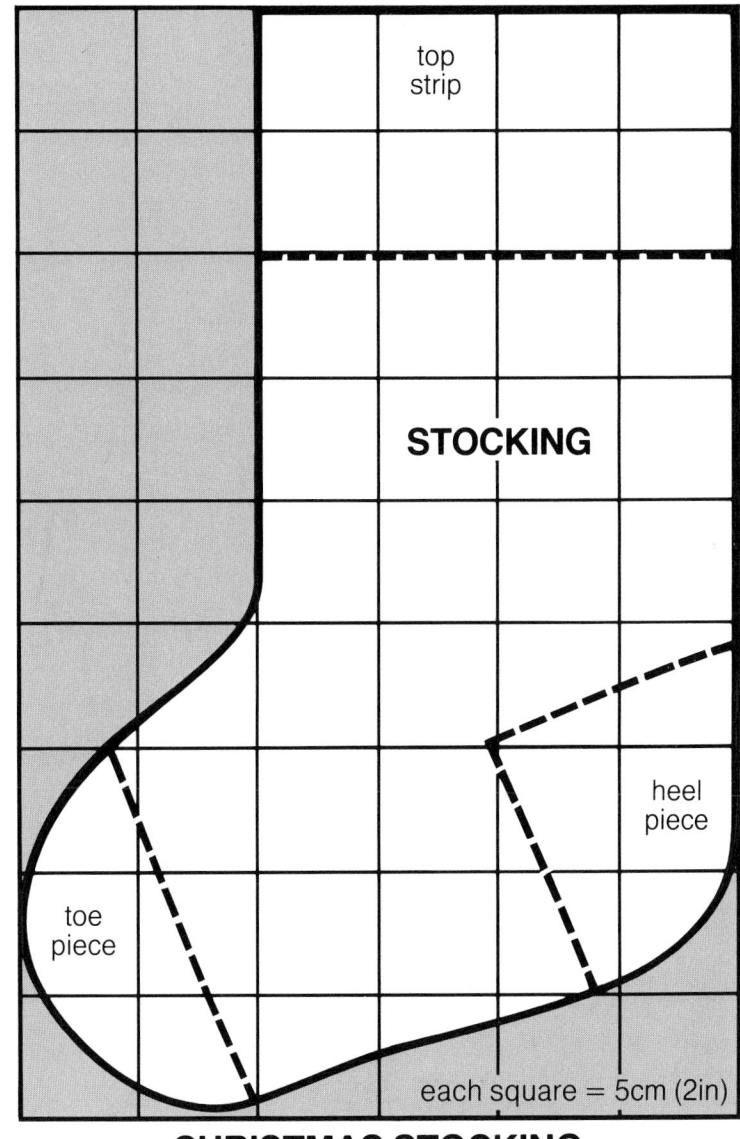

CHRISTMAS STOCKING

Make *a special Christmas stocking for each member of the family which can be used year after year. Each one is about 46cm (18in) long, so there's lots of room for presents.*

You will need: Oddments of fabrics from the rag-bag, eg cuttings off old or discarded dresses, jeans or shirts; small pieces of brightly printed fabrics; oddments of trimming and lace edging; metric or imperial graph paper (or alternatively, because the outline is so simple, you can rule a piece of paper into 5cm (2in) squares).

Notes: Copy the stocking outline from the diagram onto graph paper or ruled paper, noting that each square on diagram = 5cm (2in). Mark the dotted lines at toe, heel and top strip on your pattern. Trace these pieces separately off pattern onto paper. Seams are as stated in the instructions.

To make each stocking

Cut one pair of stocking pieces. If the fabric used is fairly thin, then cut another pair of pieces for lining from an old sheet or oddment. Tack the lining pieces to wrong side of stocking pieces.

Now, using the separate patterns, cut out one pair each of heel, toe and top pieces from the bright printed fabric. Turn in the inner edges (dotted line edges on stocking pattern) 5mm (¼in) and press.

Lay the pair of stocking pieces out, right sides up, and pin the heel and toe pieces and the top strips in position. Sew them in place. Stitch a length of trimming to the lower edge of each top strip.

Now join the stocking pieces, taking a 1cm (⅜in) seam and leaving the top edges open. Clip curves in seam and trim seam at toe and heel. Turn right side out and press.

For the hanging loop, cut a 5×15cm (2×6in) strip of printed fabric. Turn in long edges 1cm (⅜in) and press. Now stitch these long edges together with right side outside.

Hem the top edge of stocking, taking a 1cm (⅜in) turning twice, and catching the short ends of the hanging loop inside the hem at the back.

SHOPPING-BAGS

I picked up a bargain-priced curtain remnant of my favourite Liberty design in the sales and it seemed ideal for making a smart shopping-bag. For the other bag, I used the best pieces from a pair of discarded old jeans, then added a motif from the left-over bits of Liberty fabric.

The printed bag measures 34 × 39cm (13½ × 15½in) and the denim bag is a little deeper.

You will need: Cuttings from discarded denim jeans (or you can use old canvas or corduroy jeans); remnants of curtain fabric; 1.60m (1¾yd) of ric-rac braid for the denim bag.

Notes: 1cm (⅜in) seams are allowed on all pieces. Stitch the main seams twice for strength and if possible finish all the raw edges by machine zigzagging to prevent fraying.

To make the denim bag

Make the front piece first. For the centre rectangle, cut a 24×36cm (9½×14in) piece of denim. Cut a suitable motif from an oddment of curtain fabric, allowing 1cm (⅜in) all round the edge for turning. Turn in this allowance and tack in place, then press. Sew the motif to the *wrong* side of the denim rectangle. (Note that the wrong side of denim is lighter in colour than the right side and this will provide a nice contrast to the other denim strips.)

To make the side borders, cut two 8×36cm (3×14in) strips of denim. Join one long edge of each strip to one long edge of rectangle, having the raw edges level and

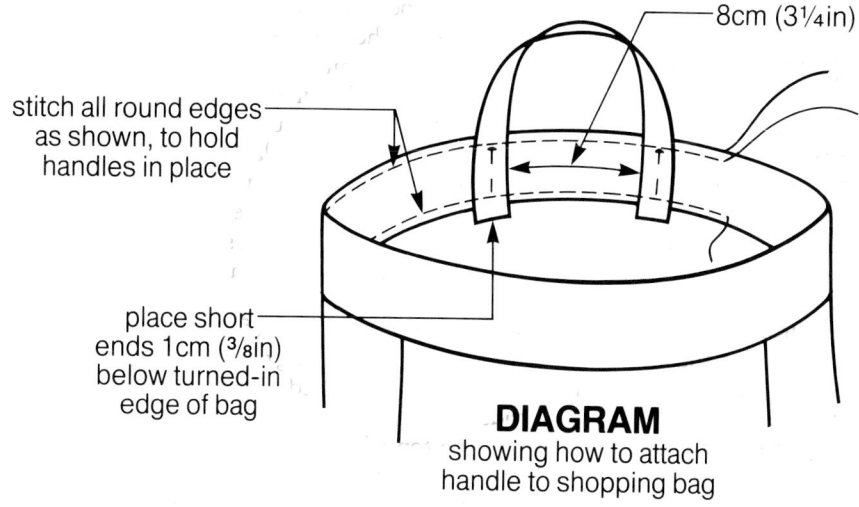

8cm (3¼in)

stitch all round edges as shown, to hold handles in place

place short ends 1cm (⅜in) below turned-in edge of bag

DIAGRAM
showing how to attach handle to shopping bag

right sides facing. Press seams open. Stitch ric-rac braid to each strip alongside the seam line.

For the lower border, cut a 6×36cm (2½×14in) strip of denim. Sew in place and add ric-rac as for the side strips.

For the top border, cut a 10×36cm (4×14in) strip of denim. Join to top edge and add ric-rac as for lower border.

For the back of the bag, cut pieces from jeans and join them as necessary, to make a rectangle the same size as front. Join front of bag to back at sides, then across lower edges. Trim seam at lower corners and leave wrong side out. Turn down top raw edge of bag 1cm (⅜in) and press, then fold this edge down to meet the top denim strip seam line and press again. Turn bag right side out.

For each handle, cut a 7×32cm (2¾×12½in) strip of denim. Turn in long edges 1cm (⅜in) and press. Fold each strip in half along length and press, having right side outside. Stitch through long edges of each handle. Oversew ends to prevent fraying.

Pin each handle inside top edge of bag as shown in the diagram. Now stitch all around the upper and lower edges of the turned in top of bag, catching handles in the stitching at the same time.

To make the printed bag

Cut two 36×44cm (14×17½in) pieces of fabric. Join them with right sides together, leaving the raw edges open at one short end. Trim seam at lower corners and leave wrong side out. Turn down top raw edge 1cm (⅜in) and press, then turn this edge down 3cm (1¼in) and press again. Turn bag right side out, then make and attach handles as for denim bag.

GUARD DOG

Hercules the hound is a super-sized draught excluder, but beware, he will almost certainly leave his post when there are children around to play with! He measures about 94cm (37in) from his front paws to his tail and is very easy to make.

You will need: 1.20m (1¼yd) of 138cm (54in) wide brown fur fabric, 700g (1½lb) of stuffing; scraps of light blue, dark blue, white and black felt; scrap of shiny black fabric for nose; a small piece of cream-coloured jersey-type fabric for the bone; metric or imperial graph paper; strong thread; adhesive.

Notes: The eye patterns are given full-size for tracing off the page. Copy the other patterns onto graph paper from the diagram (each square on diagram=5cm or 2in). 1cm (⅜in) seams are allowed on all pieces unless otherwise stated. The fur fabric pieces may be cut out with the smooth stroke of the fur pile going in any direction. When cutting a *pair* of pieces, take care to reverse the pattern when cutting out the second piece.

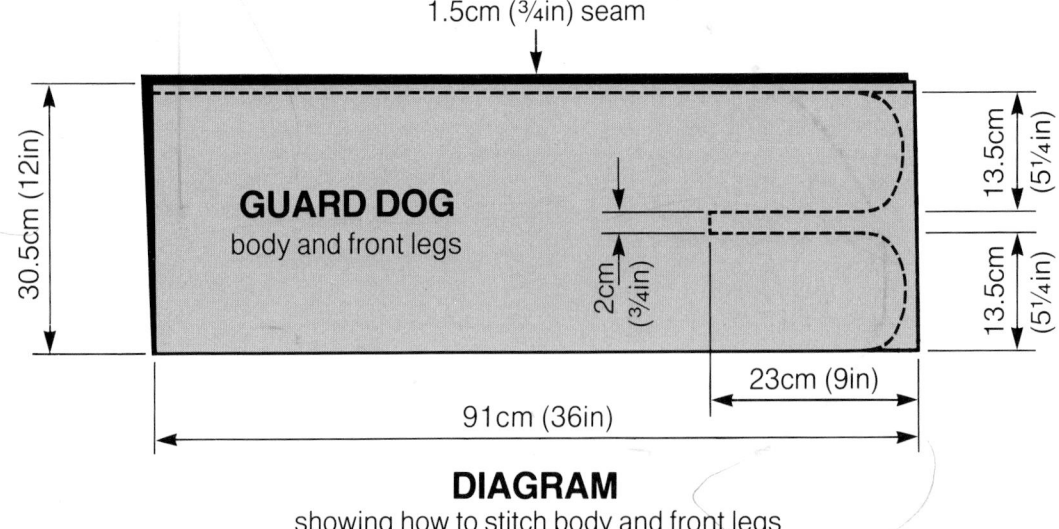

1.5cm (¾in) seam

GUARD DOG
body and front legs

30.5cm (12in)

13.5cm (5¼in)

13.5cm (5¼in)

2cm (¾in)

23cm (9in)

91cm (36in)

DIAGRAM
showing how to stitch body and front legs

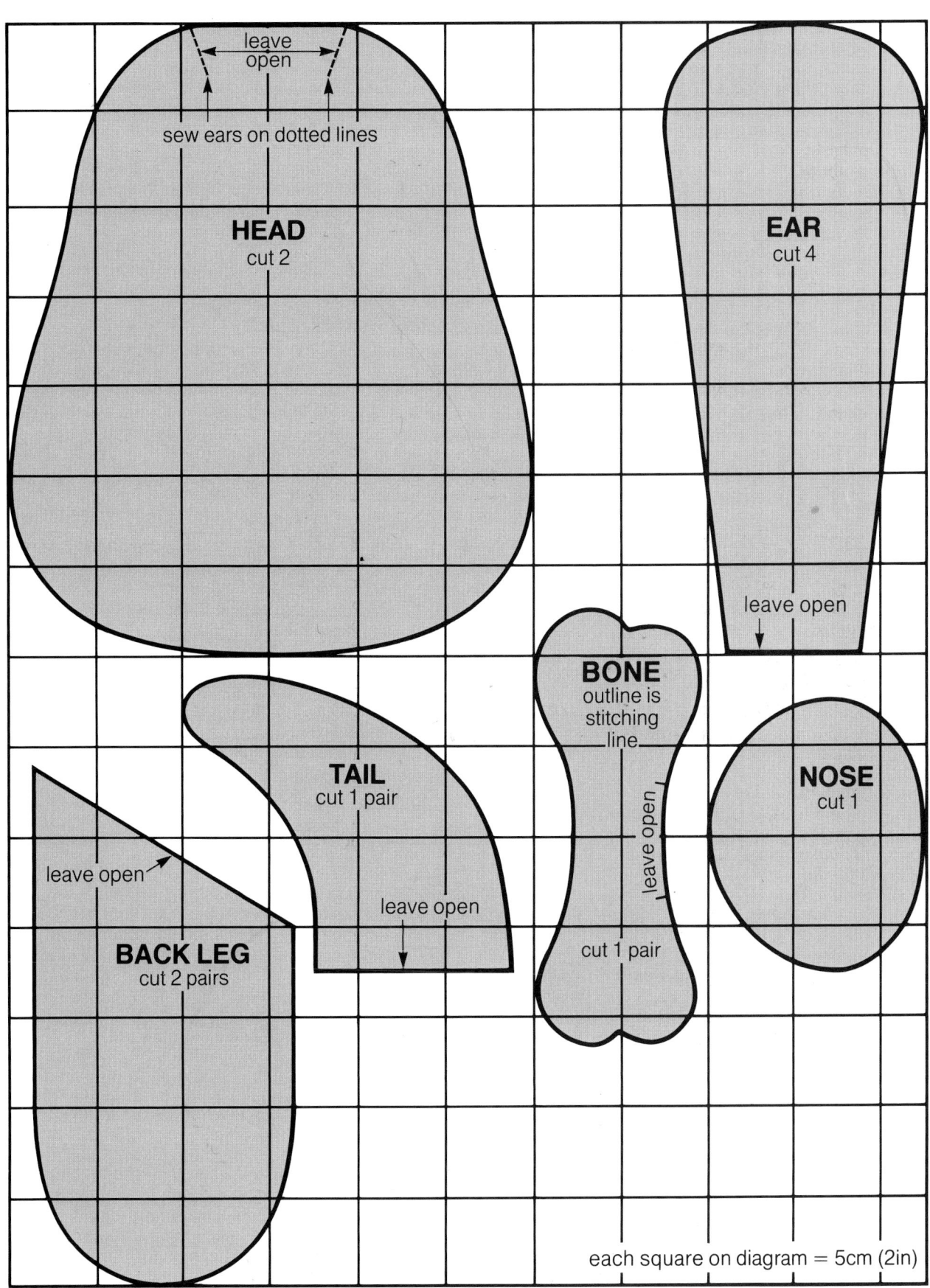

leave open

sew ears on dotted lines

HEAD
cut 2

EAR
cut 4

leave open

BONE
outline is
stitching
line

leave open

NOSE
cut 1

TAIL
cut 1 pair

leave open

cut 1 pair

leave open

leave open

BACK LEG
cut 2 pairs

each square on diagram = 5cm (2in)

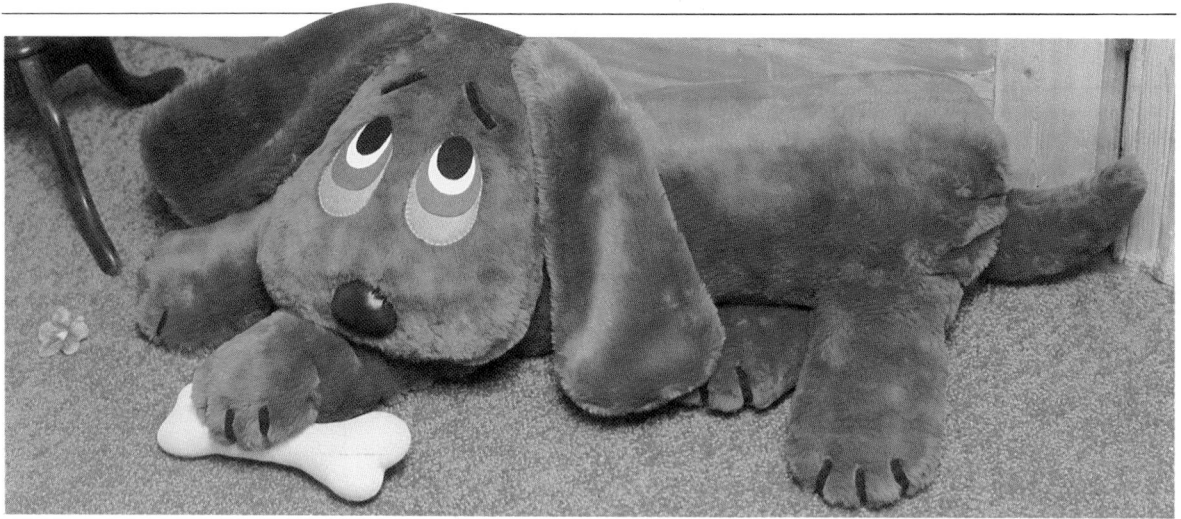

To make the dog

From the fur fabric, cut a 61×91cm (24×36in) strip for the body and front legs piece. Now using the patterns, cut out the required number of head, ear, back leg and tail pieces, from the remainder of the fur fabric. Cut out the nose piece from shiny black fabric. Cut the eye pieces from felt in the colours indicated on the full-size patterns. Do not cut out the bone pieces. Make all the separate parts of the dog before starting to assemble them.

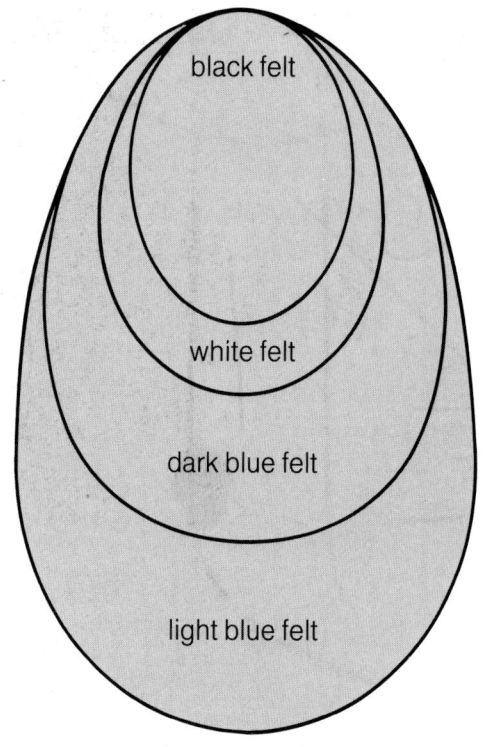

black felt

white felt

dark blue felt

light blue felt

GUARD DOG
full size eye patterns

To make the body and front legs piece, join the 91cm (36in) edges, taking a 1.5cm (¾in) seam. Mark front legs at one end of this piece with pencil to the measurements shown on the diagram, drawing around the edge of a saucer to make a smooth curve at the ends of both legs. Stitch around the marked lines through both thicknesses of fabric, then trim fabric close to stitching lines all around legs.

Turn the body and front legs piece right side out, then fill with stuffing. Run a strong gathering thread around the remaining raw edge, pull up gathers as tightly as possible, then fasten off. Oversew across gathers to completely close this end.

To make the tail, join the pieces, leaving the straight edges open, turn right side out and stuff. Turn in the seam allowance and tack, but leave the tail open at this end.

To make the back legs, join the pieces in pairs, leaving the straight edges open. Turn right side out and put a little stuffing in toe end of each leg. Oversew the raw edges of one leg together. Turn in seam allowance on raw edges of other leg and tack, but leave edges open.

Join the ear pieces in pairs, leaving the straight edges open. Turn right side out and oversew the raw edges of each ear together, pulling the stitches to gather slightly.

Now join the head pieces all around, leaving a gap in top of head, as indicated on the pattern. Turn right side out and stuff the head fairly firmly. Glue, then sew all the eye pieces together, as shown on the pattern. Sew the eyes to the face, as shown in the colour photograph. For the eyebrows, cut two 5mm×5cm (¼×2in) strips of black felt and sew one over each eye with a running stitch down the centre of each strip.

Run a gathering thread around the nose piece 1cm (⅜in) from the edge. Pull up gathers and stuff firmly, then pull up gathers tightly and fasten off. Sew the nose in position at lower edge of face, having gathers against face. Sew the tops of the ears to the head at front, as shown on the head pattern.

To assemble all the pieces

Place the body and front legs piece on a flat surface. Position the tail at the gathered end of the body with the tail resting on the flat surface. Ladder stitch the tail to body, all around the turned in edge of the tail.

Place the open-ended back leg against the side of the body at the back end, about half-way up. Ladder stitch leg to body in the same way as for the tail.

Place the other back leg underneath the body and slip stitch it in place, as in colour photograph.

Place the head on top of the body at the front, as shown in the photograph. Sew the head to the body with strong thread, working single stitches at invervals where the head touches the body.

For the paw markings, cut twelve 5mm×5cm (¼×2in) strips of black felt. Sew three on the end of each leg with a running stitch down the centre of each one.

To make the bone

Pin the pattern onto double thickness of fabric. Machine-stitch around, close to the edge of the pattern, leaving a gap in stitching, as shown on the pattern. Remove the pattern and cut out the bone close to the stitching line. Turn right side out, stuff firmly, then ladder stitch gap in seam. Place the bone under one front paw and sew it in place.

FAIRY TALE PINCUSHION

This little country scene is a sewing accessory to treasure. The tree-trunk house is designed to hold pins while the toadstools are for needles.

The base measures 11cm (4¼in) across and the tree-trunk is just over 5cm (2in) high. You can make the entire scene from scraps of suitable fabrics and felt.

You will need: Corrugated reinforced card cut off a grocery box; a cardboard tube from kitchen-towel roll or toilet-roll; scraps of green towelling, felt, fabric, shoe-lace, green fur fabric and stuffing; a few small guipure flowers; small bead for door-knob; adhesive; black and brown thread; yellow pen or pencil.

Note: There is no seaming required, the pieces are mostly glued together.

To make the base

Cut two 10cm (4in) diameter circles of card and glue them together. Spread glue on one side of the card and place it on wrong side (if your fabric has a wrong side) of a piece of green towelling. Cut out fabric about 1.5cm (⅝in) larger all round than card circle. Turn and glue this extra fabric to other side of card. Cut a circle of felt a bit smaller than base and glue it in place to cover the raw edge of fabric.

To make tree-trunk house

Cut a 5cm (2in) long section off the cardboard tube. Cut a circle of card to fit one end and glue it in place.

Cut a 7cm (2¾in) diameter circle of fawn felt and machine-stitch around it in a spiral, working towards the centre and using brown thread. Draw thread ends through to one side and knot. Stuff the card tube, then place the stitched circle right side up on top of it. While pressing firmly onto the circle to push down stuffing with one hand, glue the edge of felt circle onto side of card tube.

To cover the outside of the tree-trunk, cut a 10cm (4in) wide strip of brown fabric, long enough to go around tree-trunk plus a bit extra for an overlap. Fold strip in half along length, bringing long edges together. Glue all the raw edges together as folded. Now glue the strip around the tree-trunk, overlapping and gluing short edges.

For the door, cut a 2×3cm (¾×1¼in) piece of yellow felt and round off corners at one short edge. Sew the bead to door for the knob as shown in the colour photograph. Glue door to tree-trunk, having the short straight edge level with the base of trunk. Cut a strip of

shoe-lace to fit around the door. Neaten ends with glue, then stick it in place.

For the window, cut a 2cm (¾in) square of blue felt and round off corners slightly. Work two stitches across the centre of window both ways, using black thread to form four window-panes. Glue window to tree-trunk and add shoe-lace around edges in same way as for door.

Now spread plenty of adhesive on cardboard base of trunk and place it on the fabric-covered base in position shown in the photograph. Push pins through trunk base and into card base to hold in place until glue dries.

To make toadstools

For the larger toadstool stalk, cut a 2×14cm (¾×5½in) strip of white felt and roll it up tightly along its length. Sew end of strip in place.

For the toadstool top, cut an 8cm (3in) diameter circle of fabric (I used red, spotted with white, but plain red will do). Gather around edge of circle, then stuff firmly, pulling up gathers slightly. Push one end of stalk just inside gathers, pull up gathers around stalk, turning in the raw edge of fabric, then fasten off. Sew gathers to stalk.

Make small toadstool in same way using a 1.5×12cm (⅝×4¾in) strip of felt and a 6cm (2⅜in) diameter circle of fabric.

Glue both toadstools to the base in same way as given for tree-trunk, in positions shown in the photograph.

Finishing touches

For the path, cut three 1×1.5cm (⅜×⅝in) pieces of fawn felt. Round off corners and make edges slightly irregular also. Glue them in a row in front of door as shown in photograph.

Glue a few bits of green fur fabric to tree-trunk around base. Glue on a few guipure flowers. If you have a yellow pen or pencil handy, colour centre of each flower.

BOOKMARK BELLE

This literary lady is actually a bookmark – her head peeps out above the book to mark the correct page. She is almost 13cm (5in) high.

You will need: Scraps of thin fabric, card (postcard thickness), lace trimming, cotton wool, ribbon and felt; a wooden bead about 18mm (¾in) in diameter with a large hole; blue, red and brown fine-tipped permanent marker pens; pink nail-varnish; adhesive.

Notes: The patterns are given full-size. The body pattern is printed within the pattern for the fabric piece to show the position when making. There are no seams as all the pieces are glued together.

To make

Mark the face and the hair line on the wooden bead with an ordinary pencil, referring to the colour photograph. To steady the bead while colouring it, push the pointed end of a pencil or pen inside. Colour with marker pens and put a dot of nail-varnish on each cheek. Stand the pencil in a cup to let the head dry.

Cut the body piece from thin card, then cut out the fabric piece. Place the card in position on wrong side of fabric as shown on the pattern. Turn lower edge of fabric right over onto card and glue in place. Turn one long edge of fabric right over onto card and stick down. Repeat with the other long edge, which will lap slightly over the first edge. There is now a piece of fabric extending above the top edge of the body, which will be used to make the hat.

top edge

BOOKMARK
(fabric piece)
cut fabric the size of
rectangular outline

top edge

BOOKMARK
(body)
cut this piece
from card

lower edge

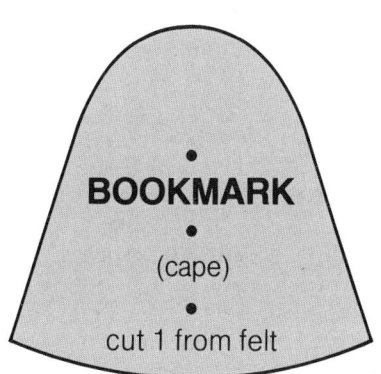

BOOKMARK

(cape)

cut 1 from felt

Push the top raw edge of this fabric right through the bead and pull the bead downwards until it rests on top of the card body. Turn in the top raw edge of fabric a little and run round a gathering thread. Stuff hat with cotton wool, then pull up gathers tightly and fasten off.

To make the hat brim, gather a 15cm (6in) strip of lace tightly round, underneath hat at top of head. Join ends of lace. Glue a ribbon bow to front of hat.

Cut the cape from felt and mark on dots for buttons. Sew the top edge of cape to fabric below head, then gather a 7cm (2¾in) length of lace around neck and fasten off.

MR AND MRS SNOWBODY

A pair of furry little toys, Mr and Mrs Snowbody stand about 18cm (7in) high without their hats. Their items of clothing are all removable, including the tiny ear-muffs which are held in place with circles of Velcro fastener.

To turn the toys into a charming Christmas table decoration, you can also make a circular tray about 32cm (12½in) across, then fill it with sweets, or decorate with a few shiny baubles and sprigs of holly.

THE DOLLS

You will need: Oddments of very short-pile, white fur fabric (Care Bears type), or if you need to buy it, 20cm (¼yd) of 138cm (54in) wide fur fabric will make five dolls; small pieces of white, black, green, orange and red felt; scrap of green fur fabric; oddments of red and green double knitting yarn (USA: worsted weight) and a pair of 3¼mm (No. 10, USA: 3) knitting-needles; scraps of red and green printed fabric, ribbon, lace trimming and narrow elastic; thin strong card; 8cm (3¼in) of white Velcro touch and close fastener; strong white thread; red pencil; a few small red beads or circles of felt; stuffing; adhesive.

Notes: Full-size patterns are given except for the pieces which are too large for the page – the body (a square), Mrs Snowbody's hat (a circle) and the tray pieces. Measurements are quoted for all these in the instructions. Seams are as stated in the instructions.

To make the basic doll

For the body and head piece, cut a 20cm (8in) square of white fur fabric. Oversew the two side edges together, making sure that the smooth stroke of the fur pile runs parallel to these edges. Leave the body wrong side out. Note when sewing on the base that the fur pile should run downwards from one raw edge (top of head) towards the other raw edge (lower edge of body).

Cut the base from card and, if necessary, glue two or three layers together to make the base quite rigid. Glue it to a piece of white felt, then cut out felt about 1cm (⅜in) larger than base all round. Run a gathering thread around edge of felt and pull gathers tightly onto the other side of card base. Fasten off gathering thread.

Slip the base inside lower edge of body, having right side of base downwards and matching the body seam to position indicated on the base pattern. Oversew the lower raw edge of body to the edge of base all round.

Turn body right side out and stuff, then gather around top edge using strong thread, pull up tightly and fasten off. Oversew across gathers to close completely. For neck, wind strong thread a couple of times around body 10cm (4in) up from base. Pull thread ends very tightly and knot. Sew thread ends into body.

Cut two pairs of arm pieces from white fur fabric, having the smooth stroke of the fur pile in direction shown on the pattern. Oversew the pieces together in pairs, leaving upper edges open. Turn right side out and stuff lightly, then oversew the raw edges of each arm together. Pin arms to sides of body, having the upper edges level with and 1.5cm (⅝in) down from the neck. Note that arms should point forwards. Sew upper edges in place.

Cut the eyes from two layers of black felt glued together. Pin them in position half-way down face and

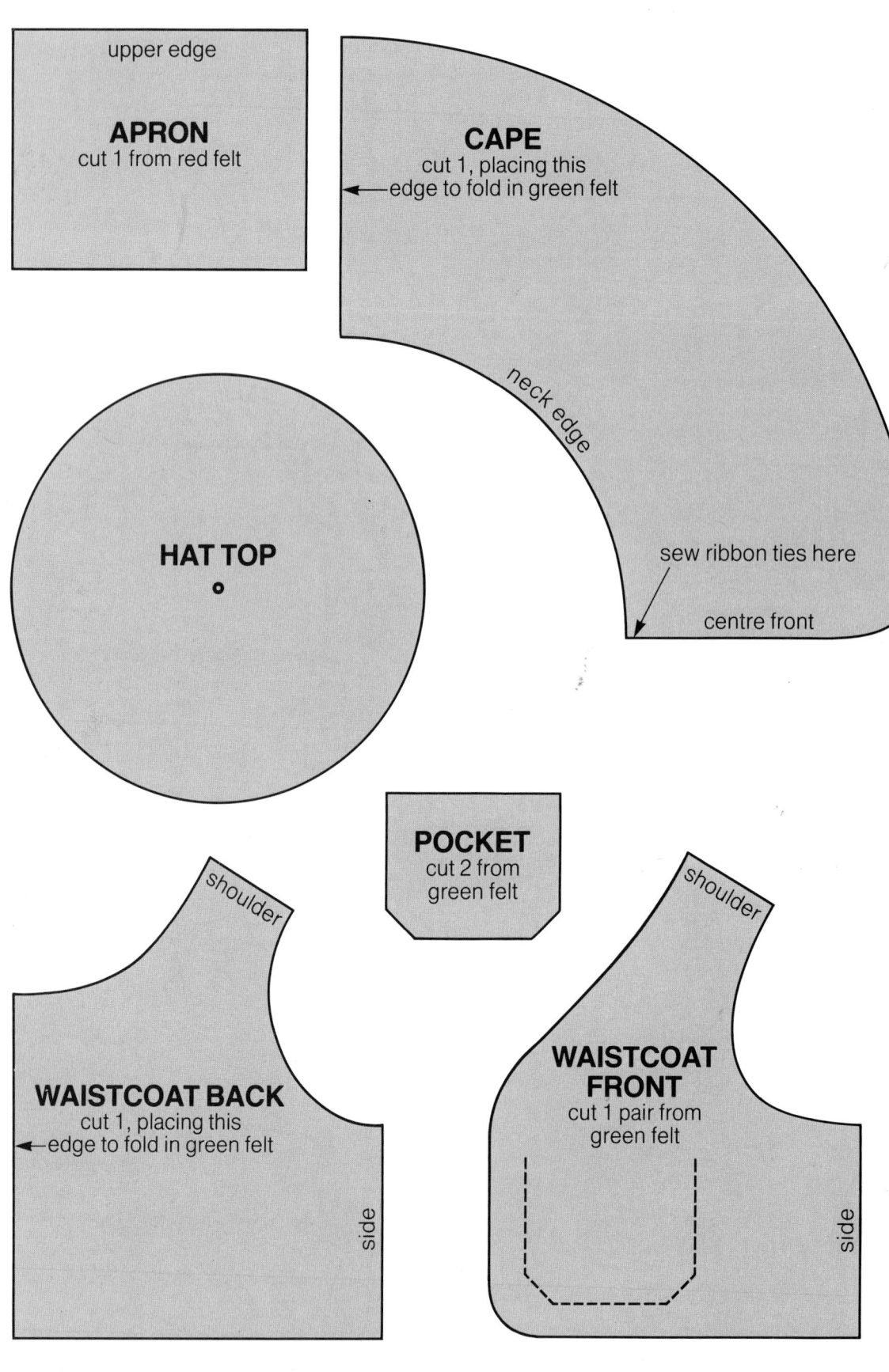

upper edge

APRON
cut 1 from red felt

CAPE
cut 1, placing this
edge to fold in green felt

neck edge

HAT TOP

sew ribbon ties here

centre front

POCKET
cut 2 from
green felt

shoulder

WAISTCOAT BACK
cut 1, placing this
edge to fold in green felt

side

shoulder

WAISTCOAT FRONT
cut 1 pair from
green felt

side

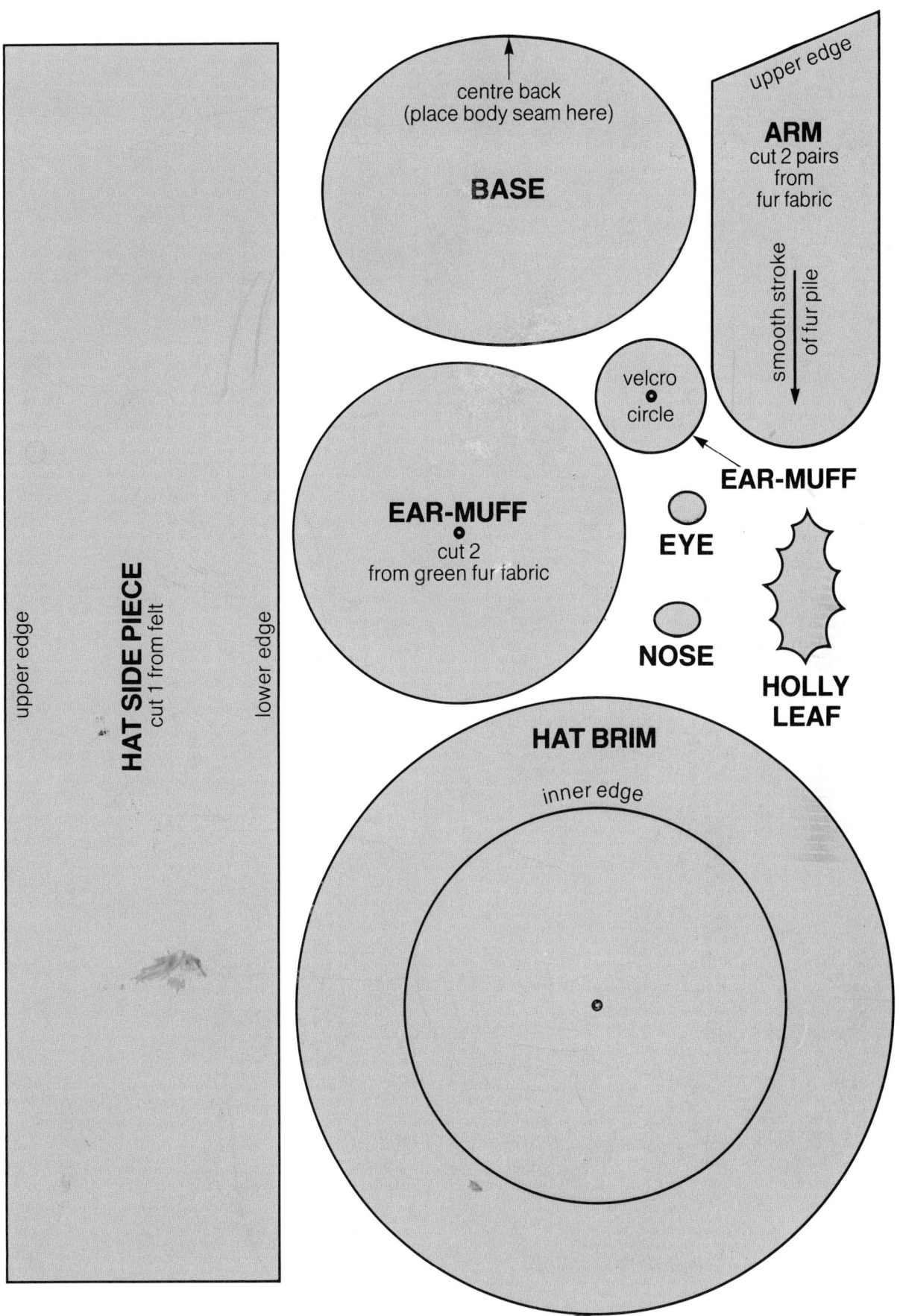

3cm (1¼in) apart. Sew them in place, taking stitches through face from centre of one eye to the other. Trim the fur pile above and at sides of eyes.

Cut the nose from three layers of orange felt glued together, then stick it in place between and just below the eyes. Colour cheeks by rubbing the fur pile with a red pencil.

MR SNOWBODY

Make the basic doll.

Ear-muffs

Cut two ear-muffs from green fur fabric. Trim the fur pile shorter all over each one. Gather round edges of circles and stuff lightly, then pull up gathers tightly and fasten off. Sew the ends of a 14cm (5½in) length of ribbon to gathered centres of circles. Cut two circles from hooked Velcro strip and sew one to each muff to cover ends of ribbon. Cut two circles from furry Velcro strip and sew them to the head at each side, so that they correspond with the ear-muff circles when the ear-muffs are in position on the doll.

Hat

Pin the hat-brim pattern to two layers of black felt, then stitch all round close to the inner and outer edges of pattern. Remove the pattern. Pull threads through to one side of felt and knot, then sew ends between layers of felt. Cut out the brim close to stitching lines.

Cut out the hat-side piece from black felt, then oversew short edges together. Now oversew lower edge of this piece to inner edge of the brim. Pin hat-top pattern to two layers of black felt, then stitch around the edge, tie off ends of thread and cut out as for brim. Oversew the hat top to the upper edge of the side piece, stretching side piece slightly to fit.

Glue ribbon around for the hat band. Cut three holly leaves from green felt and sew them to the band together with a few red beads for berries. If the toy is for a very young child, use red felt circles instead of the beads.

Scarf

Using red yarn, cast on 80 stitches and work 5 rows in garter stitch (knit every row). Cast off. Make 2 small pom-poms in green yarn and sew them to ends of scarf.

Waistcoat

Cut waistcoat fronts and back piece from green felt, as directed on patterns. Cut two pockets from green felt and sew them in position shown on front pattern. Join fronts to back at sides and shoulders, oversewing the edges together. For the handkerchief, cut a 5cm (2in) square of fabric and fray out edges. Fold, then tuck into pocket.

MRS SNOWBODY

Make the basic doll, adding ear-muffs as for Mr Snowbody.

Hat

Cut two 20cm (8in) diameter circles of printed fabric and join them around the edges, taking a 5mm (¼in) seam and leaving a gap for turning. Turn right side out and press. Stitch around the circle 2.5cm (1in) within outer edge, leaving a gap in the stitching alongside gap in outer seam. Stitch round again 5mm (¼in) within first stitching line, forming casing for elastic. Thread elastic through casing, taking it through gaps in seam and stitching line. Adjust to fit head, then join ends of elastic. Finish off gaps left in stitching line and seam. Sew ribbon bow to hat.

Apron

Cut apron from red felt and stitch lace trimming to edges except for upper edge. Stitch this edge to centre of a 35cm (14in) length of ribbon.

Cape

Cut cape from green felt as directed on pattern, then sew ribbon ties to front edges as indicated.

THE TRAY

You will need: Corrugated reinforced card cut off a grocery box. Oddments of red and green printed fabrics and green fur fabric; 1.20m (1⅜yd) of ribbon; adhesive.

To make

Cut two 30cm (12in) diameter circles of card. Glue them together, having the corrugated lines running in opposite directions for strength. Cut a 30cm (12in) diameter circle of red fabric. Cut a 5×95cm (2×37½in) strip of fur fabric, joining shorter lengths if necessary to make up the required length.

Pin one long edge of the strip around the edge of fabric circle, right sides together and having raw edges level. Trim off any excess length at ends of strip, then join the ends. Stitch the strip in place as pinned, taking a 5mm (¼in) seam.

Now spread a little glue on one side of the card circle near the edge. Place fabric circle onto it, right side up. Smooth out fabric circle so that its edge meets edge of card circle. Turn the remaining long raw edge of fur fabric strip to under side of card and glue 1cm (⅜in) of it onto card.

To decorate the tray, cut six 10cm (4in) diameter circles of green fabric. Gather round the edge of each one, pull up tightly and fasten off. Sew a red ribbon bow to the gathered centre of each circle. Sew circles to green fur fabric strip, spacing them out equally.

HANDY MANDY

T**his handy and decorative bag measures about 35.5cm (14in) from top to bottom and it can be used for holding clothes-pegs, knitting, or small items of laundry. A child's coat-hanger is inserted at the top for hooking on a washing-line or a peg in the house.**

You will need: Oddments of printed fabric, toning plain fabric for mob cap, and pink or white fabric for arms and face; scraps of brown, pink and red felt; oddments of lace trimming and narrow braid; a child-size wooden or plastic coathanger; two 1.5cm (⅝in) diameter black or brown trouser buttons; a red ball-point pen; red thread (optional).

Notes: The face and arm patterns are given full-size for tracing off the page. Seams measuring 1.3cm (½in) are allowed on all pieces unless otherwise stated.

To make the front

For the mob cap, cut a 16.5×34cm (6½×13½in) piece of plain fabric. For the dress, cut a 24×34cm (9½×13½in) piece of printed fabric. Join the pieces at one long edge and press the seam open.

Cut the face piece from pink or white fabric, placing the pattern to fold in fabric as indicated. Mark on the eye positions and the mouth. Place the face piece on top of the mob cap piece, having the lower edge of face level with the seam which joins mob cap to dress. Sew the face in place all around the edges. Sew on the buttons for eyes at the marked positions.

Trace the hair, nose and cheek patterns off the face pattern, following the dotted lines. Cut them from felt as indicated, then sew them in place. Colour the mouth with ball-point pen and mark dots above the nose for freckles. Embroider the mouth and freckles using red thread, if desired.

For the mob-cap frill, cut a 7.5×91cm (3×36in) strip of plain fabric. Hem long edges, then gather along the centre of strip so that it measures 46cm (18in). Sew the gathered centre to the top curved edge of face piece, about 5mm (¼in) away from raw edge. Stitch the frill in place again, just above first stitching line, to enclose the raw edge of face.

Pin the arm pattern onto a double thickness of pink or white fabric and trim fabric level with upper edge of pattern. Stitch all around close to the edge of the pattern, leaving upper edges open. Remove pattern, then cut out arm close to stitching line. Turn right side out and press. Make second arm in same way. Tack upper edges of arms to dress, having raw edges level with dress seam, placing each arm 4cm (1½in) in from the side edges and having thumbs pointing inwards.

For each sleeve frill, cut a 7.5×15cm (3×6in) strip of printed fabric. Hem the edges, leaving one long edge unhemmed. Gather each of these raw edges up to measure 7.5cm (3in), then stitch in place at tops of arms, having the raw edges level. Stitch the short side edges of each frill to the dress on either side of the arms. Now stitch lace trimming and narrow braid to the neck edge of the dress to cover all the raw edges.

To make the back

Cut the mob cap and dress pieces in the same way as for the front. Join them at one long edge for 7.5cm (3in) in from each end. Press seam and remaining raw edges of gap open. Hem raw edges of gap to form a neat opening.

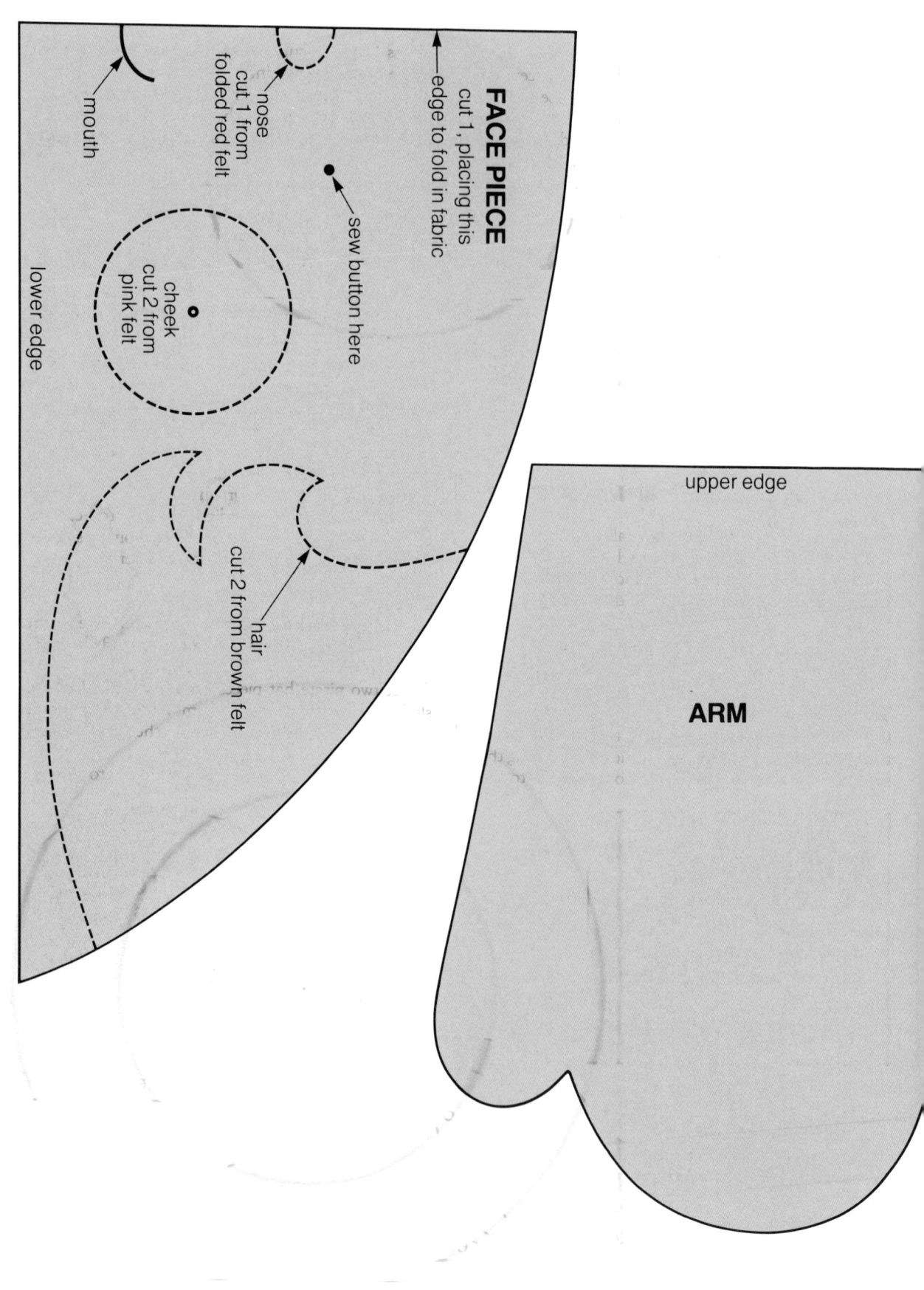

FACE PIECE
cut 1, placing this
edge to fold in fabric

nose
cut 1 from
folded red felt

mouth

sew button here

cheek
cut 2 from
pink felt

hair
cut 2 from brown felt

lower edge

upper edge

ARM

To assemble the bag

Join the front and back all around the edges except for the top edge. Leave wrong side out. Now use the top curved edge of the coathanger as a guide to draw a curve on this edge. Stitch seam as marked, leaving a tiny gap at centre for the coathanger hook. Trim off the excess fabric at curves. Turn the bag right side out. Make a bow from printed fabric and sew it to top of mob cap as illustrated in the colour photograph. Insert the coathanger through the back opening and push hook through gap in top seam.

PENCIL TOPPERS

Children will love these jolly little pencil-top characters. Each head is made from a table-tennis ball, and you only need to add bits of fabric and trimming.

You will need: One table-tennis ball for each pencil; scraps of fabric, red, black and white felt, black fur fabric, trimmings, thin card, thread, ribbon and gold braid; permanent marker pens and coloured pencils; adhesive.

Note: Patterns are printed full-size.

To make basic head

Cut the neck strip from thin card and form it into a tube by winding it tightly around the pencil, gluing the strip as you roll it up. Take care not to glue it to the pencil. Slip this cardboard tube off the pencil.

Now using sharp scissors, snip a hole in the table-tennis ball, just large enough to pass the cardboard tube through. Spread one end of the tube with glue and push it right inside ball as far as it will go, also spreading a little glue *around* the tube where it passed through the hole in the ball.

Using the colour photograph as a guide, mark on the face and hair lines with ordinary pencil. You can rub off any mistakes with an eraser. When you are satisfied with the result, colour with pens and pencils.

The pirate

Glue a small black felt patch over one eye. Glue and tie a narrow strip of fabric or ribbon around the cardboard tube for a scarf.

Cut two pirate hat pieces from black felt. Cut the skull and crossbone pieces from white felt and glue them to one hat piece, as shown on the pattern. Mark eyes on skull.

Glue centre of lower edge of front piece to front of

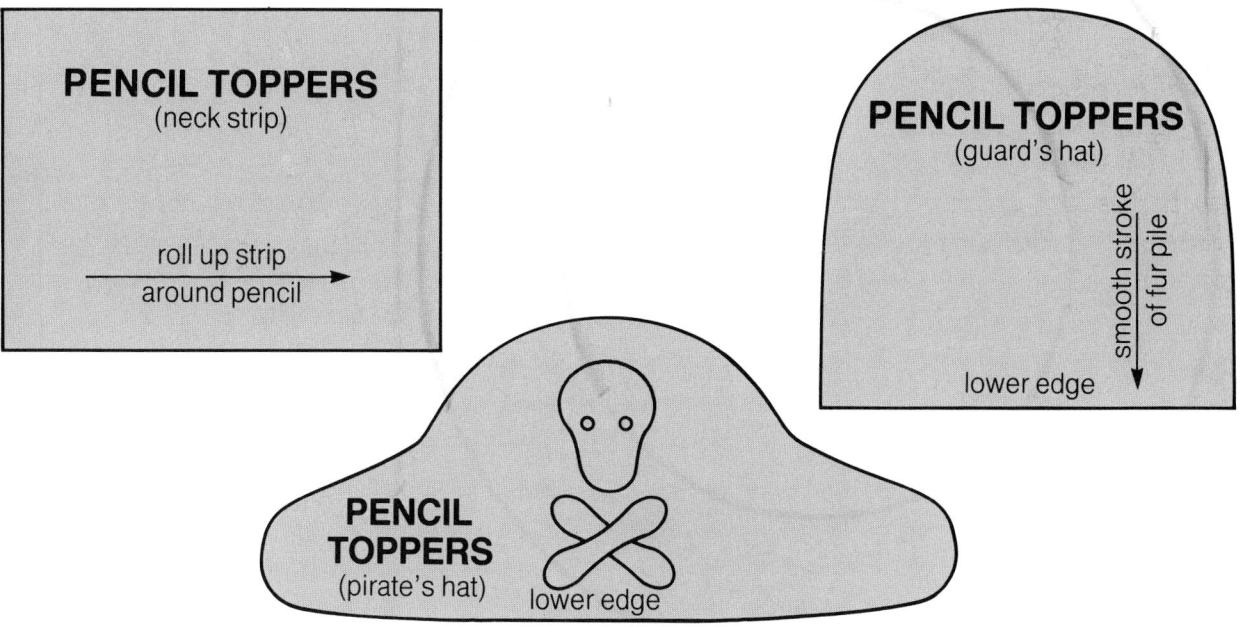

PENCIL TOPPERS
(neck strip)

→ roll up strip
around pencil →

PENCIL TOPPERS
(guard's hat)

smooth stroke of fur pile

lower edge

PENCIL TOPPERS
(pirate's hat)

lower edge

head, then glue on back in same way. Stick the hat pieces to each other at the sides.

Artist

For the cap, cut a 10cm (4in) diameter circle of fabric or felt. Run a gathering thread around the edge and pull up, leaving about a 3cm (1¼in) diameter opening at centre. Spread adhesive on the gathered edge, then stick cap in place at one side of head.

Make a tassel from a few strands of thread and sew it to centre of cap. Glue a large ribbon bow to the cardboard tube below head at front.

Guard

Glue a strip of red felt around cardboard tube to cover it, then glue a strip of narrow gold braid around it below head.

Cut a length of narrow gold braid to fit under chin and up sides of head, then stick it in place.

Cut two hat pieces from black fur fabric, having the smooth stroke of fur pile in direction shown on pattern. Oversew edges together, leaving lower edges open. Turn right side out and glue to head, lapping lower edge over ends of braid.

TINY TORTOISES

Y*ou can make these dear little creatures for the children, or use them as novelty pincushions. I only had white guipure flowers on hand for their hats, so I coloured the small* *central flowers with marker pens to tone with the body fabrics.*

They measure about 8cm (3in) from front to back.

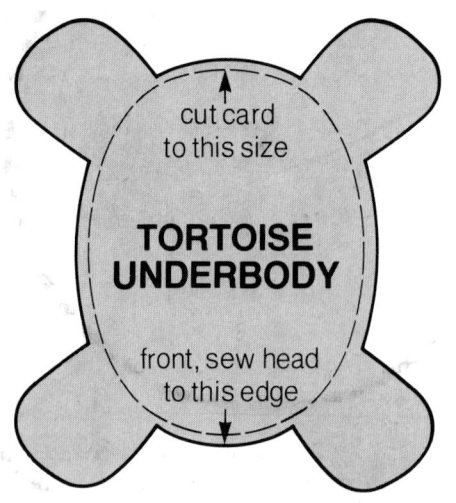

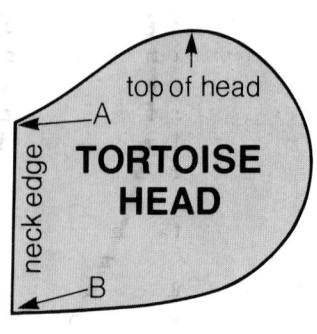

You will need: Scraps of fabric, felt, narrow ribbon, thin card and fancy braid; a small and a large guipure flower; stuffing; adhesive.

Note: Trace the underbody and head patterns onto thin paper and cut them out.

To make

For the tortoise 'shell', cut a 15cm (6in) diameter circle of fabric. Run a gathering thread around the edge and pull up gathers slightly. Stuff the circle. Cut a piece of card for the base of shell to the size of the dotted line shown on the underbody pattern. Place the card inside the gathered edge of circle, pull up gathers until the raw edges meet, then fasten off.

Pin the underbody pattern to two layers of felt. Stitch all round close to edge of pattern. Remove pattern, then draw ends of stitching threads through to one side of felt and knot them. Use needle to sew the threads neatly into underbody, between layers of felt.

Now cut out the felt close to the stitching line. Cut a small slit down the centre of *one* underbody piece, then push a little stuffing through the slit into each foot.

Having the underbody slit uppermost, place base of shell in position on top of the underbody, matching the oval shapes. Sew shell in place all around edge of fabric, leaving the feet free.

Pin the head pattern to two layers of felt, then trim the felt level with neck edge of pattern. Stitch round close to edge of pattern, leaving neck edges open. Knot ends of thread. Remove pattern and cut out head close to stitching line.

Turn head right side out and stuff firmly. Bring points marked A and B on the pattern together, then oversew across the edges, pulling stitches to gather slightly. Sew this edge to front of underbody at position shown on pattern.

Sew braid around shell at lower edge, as shown in the colour photograph. Lift up the tortoise's head and catch it to the shell with a few stitches to hold it upright. Cut two tiny circles of black felt (use leather punch if available) and glue them in place for eyes as illustrated.

Take a strip of ribbon under tortoise's chin and join ends at top of head. Sew large guipure flower to the ribbon join, with small flower at centre.

SEWING SUSAN

This demure little lady is about 13cm (5in) tall and she is designed to keep together all those bits and pieces which are required for hand-sewing.

Her hat is used as a pincushion and the pocketed apron holds needles, a threader and skein of various coloured sewing threads. As a finishing touch, I added a thimble handbag, but this can be omitted if cost is an important factor.

However, if the doll is to be made for a special gift, then a small pair of pretty needlework scissors could be included also, and instructions are given accordingly.

For the doll you will need: Oddments of printed and plain fabric, ribbon, lace edging, narrow ric-rac, guipure flowers or other trimming, flesh-coloured and one other colour of felt, stuffing, thin strong card; brown embroidery thread; red pencil; adhesive.
For the sewing accessories you will need: Needle threader; sewing needles; coloured sewing threads; pins; thimble and needlework scissors (both optional).

Notes: Only one pattern is required (for the hand), and this is printed full-size. All other pieces are rectangles or circles for which measurements are given. Seams measuring 5mm (¼in) are allowed unless otherwise stated.

The doll

For the base, cut an 8cm (3in) diameter circle of card, gluing several layers together, if necessary, for strength. For the skirt, cut a 10 × 26cm (4 × 10in) strip of printed fabric. Join short edges of strip. Turn skirt right side out.

Slip the card circle just inside the raw edge of fabric at one end. Glue the raw edge 1cm (⅜in) onto the card all round the circle. Cover this raw edge by gluing a slightly smaller circle of felt to the base.

Stuff the skirt, then turn in the remaining raw edge, run round a gathering thread and pull up gathers slightly. Continue stuffing to fill skirt completely, but do not fasten off gathers. Glue lace and ric-rac around lower edge of skirt, as shown in the colour photograph.

For the body and head piece, cut a 7cm (2¾in) square of flesh-coloured felt. Join two opposite edges. Leaving the piece wrong side out, gather round one remaining edge, pull up gathers tightly, then fasten off. Turn right side out and stuff.

To form the neck, tie strong thread tightly around the felt 3cm (1⅛in) away from gathered end. After knotting, sew thread ends into neck.

For the dress bodice, cut a 4 × 8.5cm (1⅝ × 3⅜in) strip of printed fabric. Join the short edges, then turn right side out. Turn in one remaining raw edge and run round a gathering thread. Put the bodice on the doll, having gathers around the neck and matching seam on fabric to centre back seam on doll. Pull up gathers tightly and fasten off. Tack the remaining raw edge of fabric to lower edge of body.

Slip this edge of body 1cm (⅜in) inside gathered edge of skirt. Pull up skirt gathers tightly around body, taking care that skirt seam is in line with bodice seam. Fasten off, then sew gathered edge of skirt to body.

For the eyes, use double black thread to work a small vertical stitch for each eye, starting and fastening off thread at back of head where it will be hidden by hat. Use red thread to work a small V-shape for mouth in same way. Colour cheeks and mark on a dot for nose, using a red pencil.

For the hair, cut twelve 14cm (5½in) lengths of brown embroidery thread. Back stitch centres of lengths to front of head at 'centre-parting' line. Bring strands of thread to each side of head and catch them to head in bunches, about level with mouth. Fold strands upwards, taking them to top of head at back. Sew them there and trim off any excess length.

The hat

For hat brim, cut a 3 × 18cm (1¼ × 7in) strip of plain fabric. Join short ends of strip, then fold one long raw edge up to meet the other, having right side of fabric outside. Gather round the raw edges, then pull up gathers so that brim fits on back of head, as shown in the photograph. Fasten off, then sew gathers to head.

For top of hat, cut a 6cm (2½in) diameter circle of plain fabric, gather round edge, then pull up gathers slightly and stuff circle. Pull up gathers more tightly and fasten off, but leave a small hole at centre of gathers.

Push top of hat, gathered side down, onto hat brim gathers. Use the point of a needle to turn in the raw edge of circle, then pin gathered edge of hat in place. Ladder stitch to head as pinned. Sew a ribbon bow to front of hat.

back, then use one of the ribbon loops on the bow for slipping the needlework scissors through.

The sleeves

For each sleeve, cut a 5cm (2in) square of printed fabric. Join two opposite edges of each square, then turn them right side out.

Turn in one remaining raw edge of each sleeve, then oversew edges together, pulling stitches to gather slightly.

For each hand, cut two pieces from flesh-coloured felt, using the pattern. Oversew the pieces together in pairs around the edges, leaving wrist edges open. Turn right side out and put a little stuffing in each one.

wrist edge

HAND

Stuff sleeves lightly. Turn in the remaining raw edge of each one and run round a gathering thread. Push a hand just inside the gathered edge of each sleeve, pull up gathers to fit, fasten off, then sew to hands. Sew gathered tops of sleeves to sides of doll, just below neck.

The thimble basket

For the basket, cut a 6cm (2⅜in) length of 2cm (¾in) wide lace edging. Join ends and turn right side out. For base of basket, cut a 1.5cm (⅝in) diameter circle of card, then slip it just inside straight edge of lace edging. Glue this edge just onto card base all round. Glue a circle of felt to base to cover this edge of lace.

Sew on a length of ribbon for a handle, as shown in the photograph, adding a guipure flower to each end if you are using this kind of trimming. Sew ribbon handle to doll's hand. Now catch the basket to skirt where it touches, to keep it steady while in use. Bend the other arm slightly, then sew hand to skirt.

The sewing accessories

Stick pins into the hat – the glass-headed variety look best. Put the needle threader into one of the pockets and attach a couple of different sized sewing needles through felt on outside of pocket. Place thimble in the basket. Slip scissors through ribbon loop, if using.

To make the skein of sewing threads, cut about thirty 30cm (12in) lengths of various coloured threads. Fold them all in half, then get someone to hold all the folded ends around one finger, while you plait the threads together. To prevent the plait unravelling, knot a strand of sewing thread around the end of the plait. Each strand of thread may now be drawn out of the plait from the folded end, as required.

The apron

Cut a 7×9cm (2¾×3½in) piece of coloured felt. Fold up one short edge 2.5cm (1in) and press, to form the pockets. Stitch along sides to hold this folded up section in place, then stitch up centre, to divide into two separate pockets. Sew trimming to side and lower edge of the apron. Gather along the remaining edge and pull up to fit front waist of doll, then fasten off. Sew this edge to bodice where skirt meets it.

Cut a length of ribbon to fit around the waist, having it long enough to tie in a bow at the back. Tie ribbon in position, putting a spot of glue at centre front to hold in place. Sew the bow securely to bodice at

DOLLY DUSTERS

The prettiest way to package cleaning cloths and dusters for fund-raising is to turn them into dolls. These dolls are often fashioned around a wooden spoon, with the bowl of the spoon forming the head.

Here is another version of a doll which is almost as quick to make, because the cloths are held together with rubber hands. An odd stitch or two is required and these can be snipped when the dolls are taken apart for use. The finished dolls are about 28cm (11in) tall and each one provides three or four household cloths. A wire scouring-pad forms the golden hair of one of the dolls and the handbag is a little lavender sachet.

For the basic cone-shape over which the dolls are made you will need: Any kind of waste paper or card such as newspaper, magazines, brown wrapping-paper, remnants of wallpaper or thin card cut off household packages.

You will also need: Newspaper and paper tissues for stuffing the heads; 'Goldilocks' scouring-pads; yellow dusters; plain stockinette dish-cloths; all-purpose cleaning cloths (such as 'J-cloths'); woven dish-cloths; towelling face flannels; assorted sizes of rubber bands; sticky tape; scraps of ribbon, printed fabric, brown knitting yarn; string; lavender flowers; red thread; brown marker pen; for the eyes, self-adhesive labels in black and blue about 7mm (5/16in) in diameter; red pencil; brown pen; adhesive.

Notes: You should shop around for the cloths, as prices do vary considerably. Best buys are packaged in bulk, from chain stores, market stalls and supermarkets. Iron all the cloths to take out creases before starting.

Where any items are sewn in place, use only a couple of large stitches so that they can be snipped easily when dolls are taken apart. Each head is made from a plain stockinette dish-cloth, stuffed with newspaper.

The cone-shaped body
The dolls are based on a simple cone-shaped body and the pattern for this is too large for the page and also outside the span of normal compasses. However, it can be drawn quite easily in the following way.

First, cut a 24cm (9½in) square of paper. Now use ruler and pencil to mark short lines at intervals, measuring 24cm (9½in) from one corner each time as shown in Diagram 1. The diagram shows a metric ruler, but you can use imperial instead. Use compasses (or ruler as before) to mark a curve in the same way, 6cm (2⅜in) away from the same corner as shown in the diagram. Cut out the paper pattern through the marked lines.

Now draw around the pattern onto paper or card as available, then cut out along marked lines. Note that if using newspaper or magazines you will need to cut the body from about ten layers, or four layers of brown wrapping-paper, or only one thickness of card. Use your own judgement as to how many layers you will need to make a rigid cone.

DOLL WITH HANDBAG

For the head, take one page of newspaper and crumple it up, rolling up all the corners towards the centre until you have a flattish rounded shape which is as smooth as possible at the front (see Diagram 2). If you wish, you can now put a couple of layers of paper tissue over the front of the shape so that crumples do not show through the cloth, but this is not essential.

Now take one stockinette dish-cloth and fold it in half or into quarters, according to how large it is. Place smooth side of newspaper ball at centre, then gather the cloth around paper to enclose it. Pull corners of cloth towards edge of ball and secure with a rubber band, as shown in Diagram 3. You may find there are gaps showing the newspaper ball, but this does not matter so long as the smooth front is covered. Mould the newspaper ball within the cloth to smooth out any crinkles which may be showing through the cloth.

Form the cut-out body shape into a cone, at the same time enclosing the gathered edges of head (just below rubber band) at the narrow end of cone. Overlap the long straight edges of cone and secure them with bits of sticky tape.

For the dress, take an all-purpose cloth and fold it in half, bringing the short edges together (cloths are usually oblong in shape) and press the fold. Wrap cloth around doll with both short edges level with lower edge of cone and folded edge extending above doll's head. Position the other edges of the cloth at back of doll. Now secure a small rubber band around the cloth at position of doll's neck. Space out the gathers evenly.

Turn the folded edge which is above doll's head right down onto cone. Place a larger rubber band around this portion to represent the doll's waist. There will now be a frill of cloth below the rubber band, as you can see in the colour photograph (overleaf).

For the doll's arms, you need to cut up a plain stockinette cloth, but you should be able to get four or five such strips from one cloth to make arms for several dolls. Cut an 8cm (3in) wide strip across the full width of the cloth. Fold both long raw edges to the centre of the strip, then fold the strip in half down its length so that the long raw edges are enclosed. Tie a length of sewing thread tightly around the centre of the strip. Lay this piece aside for now.

For the handbag, cut a 14cm (5½in) diameter circle from a bit of printed fabric. Turn in the raw edge 1cm (⅜in) and gather around the circle through double thickness close to the *raw* edge. Fill with lavender flowers, then pull up gathers tightly, enclosing a loop of ribbon for the handle. Fasten off, then sew through gathers to hold ribbon in place.

Slip the handbag onto the arms piece, then tuck short ends of arms piece into elastic band at back of doll's waist so that handbag is at the front.

For the cape, take a yellow duster and wrap it around doll, with one long edge of the duster level with base of cone, (opposite edge of duster will extend above doll's head). Secure the duster around doll's neck with a rubber band. Adjust gathers evenly and make sure lower edge is level with lower edge of cone all round.

Fold back the edge of the duster which is above doll's head, about 2cm (¾in). Let the centre of this folded edge rest across and down the sides of doll's head. Secure this portion of duster round the doll's neck again with a rubber band. Adjust folded edge of duster to leave it folded over the head, but straighten out the fold below the elastic band. There will now be a bit of duster below elastic band at each side of front, which looks like a shorter cape, as you can see in the photograph. Adjust gathers again and smooth these short cape pieces downwards.

Pull the hood gently backwards off doll's head. Work a V-shape for mouth in red thread, taking needle through from back of head. For the eyes, cut one blue label in half before peeling it off the backing paper. Peel off and stick each half to a black label. Peel black labels off paper and place them on face. Colour cheeks and a dot for nose with a red pencil.

Put the scouring-pad on doll's head, easing strands apart at centre to make it fit. Ease the hood back in position over the scouring-pad. Catch a ribbon bow to neck of dress at front with a stitch or two.

CINDERELLA DOLL

Make the head, cone, dress and arms as for the other doll, working an inverted V-shape for mouth. For the shawl, use a woven dish-cloth and attach it around doll's neck at centre with a rubber band, then fold down the upper half which is above rubber band. Use large stitches to sew a few printed fabric patches to shawl and dress. Tie a string bow around the neck.

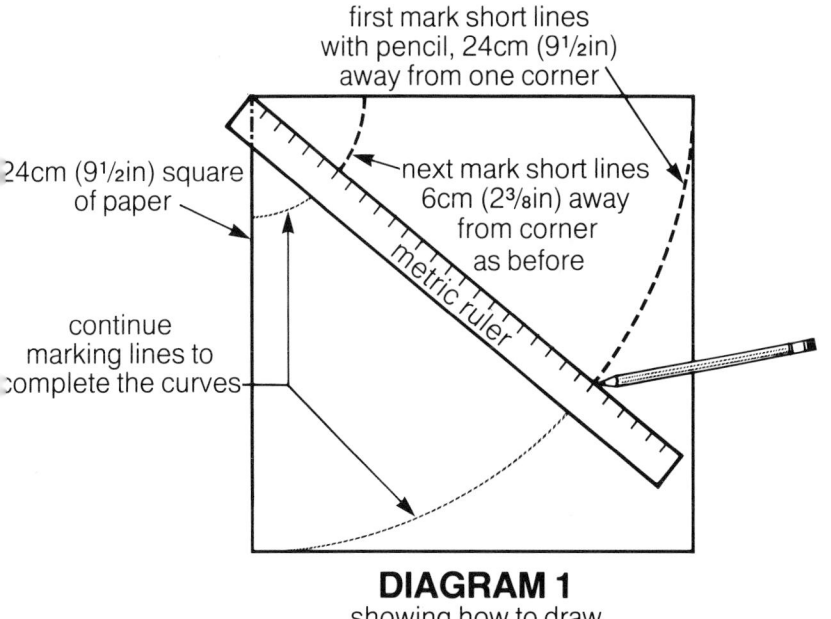

first mark short lines with pencil, 24cm (9½in) away from one corner

next mark short lines 6cm (2⅜in) away from corner as before

24cm (9½in) square of paper

metric ruler

continue marking lines to complete the curves

DIAGRAM 1
showing how to draw the cone-shaped body pattern

DIAGRAM 2

side view of crumpled newspaper, used to shape doll's head

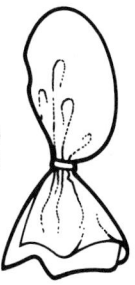

DIAGRAM 3

cover newspaper with folded cloth, and hold gathers in place with a rubber band

For hair, cut fourteen 24cm (9½in) lengths of knitting yarn. Sew centres to forehead and catch strands to each side of head. For a headscarf, use a face flannel. Fold it diagonally and place fold across top of head. Take all corners to the back and catch them together. Catch scarf to head at each side.

For the broom handle, cut a 6×14cm (2½×5½in) strip of brown paper. Roll it up across the width around a thin knitting-needle. Glue the long edge in place. Slide handle off needle, then colour randomly with a brown pen.

For bristles, cut a 6×30cm (2¼×12in) strip of brown paper and colour it as for handle. Snip at intervals all along one edge, leaving 1cm (⅜in) at the other long edge uncut. Wind and glue this bit around one end of handle. Glue handle to inside of Cinderella's hands.

A BASKET FULL OF STRAWBERRIES

Choose a pretty quilted fabric and some narrow lace trimming to make the basket, then cram it with satiny lavender-filled strawberries. The basket measures 10cm (4in) high, including the handle, and is simply made from two circles, pulled to shape with elastic. Five or six strawberries will fill the basket, or you can make the fruit singly to hang in a wardrobe or scent a drawer.

For the basket you will need: Small pieces of quilted fabric; 90cm (1yd) of 1.5cm (⅝in) wide lace edging; short lengths of ribbon and elastic.

For the strawberries you will need: Small pieces of shiny red fabric such as taffeta or satin; green felt and narrow

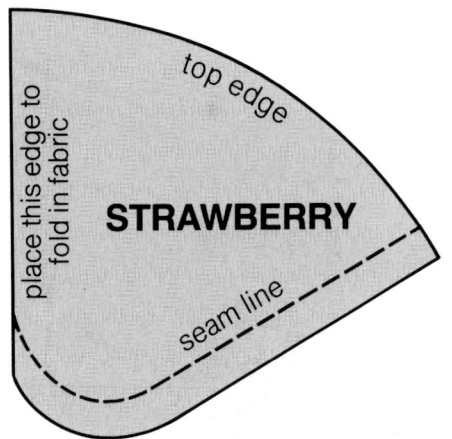

place this edge to fold in fabric

top edge

STRAWBERRY

seam line

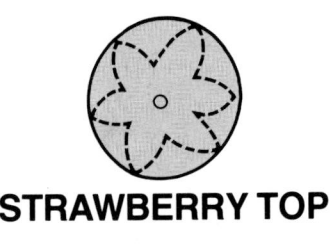

STRAWBERRY TOP

green ribbon; dried lavender flowers; fine-tipped black permanent marker pen; adhesive.

Notes: The patterns for the strawberries are given full-size. Take 5mm (¼in) seams unless otherwise stated.

To make the basket

Cut two 16cm (6¼in) diameter circles of quilted fabric. On the right side of one circle sew the straight edge of the lace level with edge of circle, having the fancy edge of lace pointing towards centre of circle. Now join both circles around the edges, having right sides together, sandwiching lace between them and leaving a gap for turning.

Turn right side out. Turn in the raw edges of gap and slip stitch, but leave a tiny gap for inserting the elastic. Now stitch all around the circle 1cm (⅜in) away from edge of quilted fabric. Thread elastic through opening, pulling it up tightly to form the basket shape. Join ends of elastic and slip stitch gap.

For the basket handle, cut two 3×18cm (1¼×7in) strips of quilted fabric. Sew lace to the long edges of one strip in same way as for basket. Join strips at long edges, sandwiching lace between them as for basket.

Oversew the raw edges at one end together, then turn handle right side out by pushing this end through with a knitting-needle. Turn in the raw edges of fabric at the ends and slip stitch. Sew ends of handle to each side of basket, level with stitching line below elastic. Sew a ribbon bow to each end of handle.

To make the strawberries

Cut the strawberry from fabric, placing edge of pattern indicated to fold in fabric. Keeping fabric folded, stitch seam as shown on pattern. Turn right side out and run round a gathering thread 5mm (¼in) away from top raw edge.

Fill with lavender, then pull up gathers tightly, turning in the raw edges and pushing in the ends of a 7cm (2¾in) length of green ribbon to form a loop. Fasten off, then sew through gathers and ribbon to hold in place.

Mark the strawberry with dots using a marker pen, as shown in the colour photograph. Cut a rough circle of green felt for the strawberry top, then cut a tiny hole at centre. Snip the circle to shape as shown on the pattern. Use tweezers or a pin to pull the ribbon loop on the strawberry, through centre hole in felt. Stick felt to strawberry with a dot of glue.

HEART AND FLOWER SACHETS

Pretty fabric sachets filled with lavender or pot-pourri are perennial best-sellers at bazaars and sales of work. The flower is about 10cm (4in) across and the heart measures 9cm (3½in) from top to bottom.

You will need: Scraps of thin printed and plain fabrics, ribbon, lace trimming and light-weight iron-on interfacing; lavender flowers or pot-pourri.

Notes: Patterns are given full-size. For the flower sachet, the two patterns required overlay each other. First trace off the flower around the petal outline, then cut it out. Now trace off the outer circle around the dotted line and mark on the inner dotted circle also. Cut out pattern around the outer circle, then cut away the inner circle and discard it. Seams are as stated in the instructions.

To make the heart-shaped sachet

Cut one piece from plain and one from printed fabric, placing the edge of the pattern indicated to fold in fabric each time. Open up the folded pieces, then cut a slit across the plain fabric piece, as shown on the pattern.

Pin straight edge of lace trimming around the edge of one piece on right side, having the straight edge of lace and raw edge of fabric level. Ease lace around corners and points and have fancy edge of lace pointing inwards. Tack as pinned.

Now place the two pieces together with right sides facing and sandwiching lace between them. Stitch all around the edges, taking a tiny seam. Turn right side out through slit.

Put a little lavender or pot-pourri into sachet through slit and shake some into each of the points. Catch the raw edges of slit together.

Now fold down one point so that the slit is at the fold on the inside. Run a gathering thread through the folded edge, as shown on the pattern. Pull up the gathers tightly and fasten off.

Tie a ribbon bow, leaving long ends. Sew the bow to gathers with long ends at top. Sew ribbon ends to back of gathers, forming loops.

To make the flower-shaped sachet

Iron the interfacing on to wrong side of a piece of printed fabric to stiffen it. Place the stiffened fabric on a piece of unstiffened printed fabric, having right sides together. Pin flower petal pattern to the two layers.

Now stitch all round, close to edge of pattern. Remove pattern and cut out the flower shape 3mm (⅛in) away from the stitching line. Clip seam at all the corners between petals.

Cut a slit across the centre of the unstiffened piece of fabric only, as shown on the pattern. Turn flower right side out through the slit, ease out all the petals, then press.

Using the other circular pattern, cut out a piece of plain fabric. While the pattern is still pinned to fabric, mark the edge of the inner cut-out circle on the fabric. Pin the plain fabric circle marked side uppermost, centrally on the slit side of the flower. Using double thread, gather around the marked circle through all the thicknesses. Pull up the gathers slightly to form a cup shape at flower centre, then fasten off.

Turn in the raw edge of plain fabric circle 5mm (¼in) and gather round it. Pull up gathers slightly. Fill the cupped centre of flower with lavender or pot-pourri.

Cut a 10cm (4in) length of ribbon and form it into a double loop. Push ribbon ends into centre of gathers, pull up gathers tightly and fasten off, then sew through gathers and ribbon.

Cut a 10cm (4in) length of lace and join the ends. Run a gathering thread along one long edge, then pull up gathers tightly around the ribbon loops and fasten off. Catch lace to ribbon.

Sew a loop of ribbon to back of flower for hanging it up.

Photograph on page 72

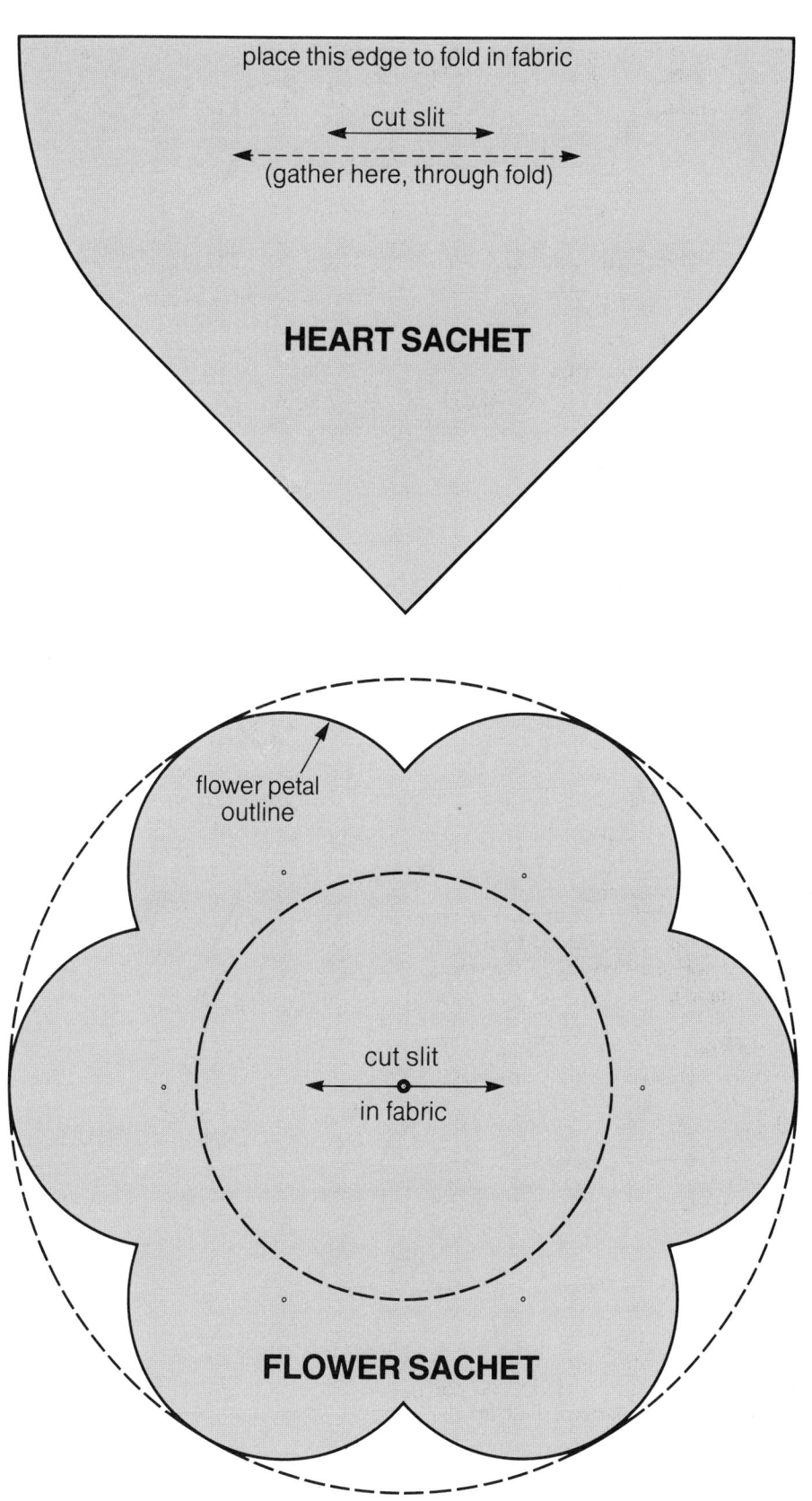

place this edge to fold in fabric

cut slit

(gather here, through fold)

HEART SACHET

flower petal
outline

cut slit
in fabric

FLOWER SACHET

Heart and flower sachets (see page 70)

BRING ON THE CLOWNS

All three clowns are made from pretty Liberty lawn and here is an instance where this fabric can be used quite economically – for the smallest (a brooch), 10cm (4in) of fabric will make five clowns, working out at only a few pence each.

The middle-sized clown is a lavender sachet, the largest is a toy or mascot. The height of each one in order is: 6.5cm (2½in), 9cm (3½in) and 14cm (5½in). A wooden bead is used for each head – the actual size is not crucial, use the nearest size available to that quoted in the instructions.

For all three clowns you will need: Scraps of thin fabric, fur fabric, coloured felt for the feet; flesh-coloured felt, ribbon, narrow tape, narrow ric-rac and braid trimmings; small coloured beads; Copydex (latex-type adhesive); adhesive (UHU type); red and blue fine-tipped permanent marker pens; pink nail-varnish; stuffing.

In addition you will need: For the brooch: a 15mm (⅝in) diameter wooden bead and small safety-pin; for the sachet: an 18mm (¹¹⁄₁₆) diameter wooden bead and lavender flowers; for the toy: a 28mm (1⅛in) diameter wooden bead.

Notes: Patterns are all printed full-size for tracing off the page. Seams and turnings are as stated in the instructions.

To make the brooch

First prepare the flesh-coloured and the coloured felt pieces by spreading them generously with Copydex and sticking two layers together. Leave to dry, then iron the felt pieces on both sides with a hot iron over a damp cloth. Cut the feet and hands from felt using the appropriate colours and patterns, then lay them aside for now.

Cut a short length of tape and push one end through the bead. Turn down this end and glue it onto bead as shown in Diagram 1.

Cut two body pieces from fabric. Turn in all the raw edges of each 1cm (⅜in) and press. Oversew the squares together at two opposite edges for half-way down only, as shown in Diagram 2. These seams will be at the centre front and back of body.

Bring these seams together, then oversew the remainder of the edges together, as shown in Diagram 3, to form the legs. Turn the body right side out.

Gather around the neck edge, then pull up gathers tightly around the length of tape just below the head. Fasten off, then sew tape to gathers. Stuff body and legs lightly through lower edges of legs. Run gathering threads around these edges and pull up slightly. Slip the feet inside them, having the dotted line shown on the pattern level with gathered edges of fabric. Pull up gathers, fasten off, then sew in place through the feet.

Cut one arms piece from fabric. Turn in all the raw edges and press, as for body. Oversew the long edges

Although there are only nine squares on the board, you will need to make five noughts and five crosses – don't forget, the loser will have one left over! The padded board is 24cm (9⅜in) square.

You will need: Small oddments of plain and printed fabrics; thin polyester wadding and a little stuffing; 2m (2¼yd) of narrow braid or ric-rac trimming; an 18cm (7in) strip of hooked Velcro fastener in colour to tone with board; a 10cm (4in) strip of furry Velcro fastener in colour to tone with noughts and the same for the crosses.

Notes: Trace the nought and cross patterns off the page onto thin paper and also trace off the large dots and the lines across centres. Cut out the patterns. Seams are as stated in the instructions.

To make the board

Draw a 24cm (9⅜in) square onto a piece of plain fabric, having straight weave of fabric in line with edges of square. Mark two lines 8cm (3⅛in) apart each way across the square to divide it into nine equal squares.

Cut out the fabric 1cm (⅜in) larger all round than the 24cm (9⅜in) square. Sew braid to all the marked lines *except for* the original outer square.

For the underside of the board, cut a 26cm (10⅛in) square of plain fabric and also of wadding. Place the braid-trimmed square right side up on top of the wadding square, then place the other square on top of this.

Join all the pieces around the edges, taking a 1cm (⅜in) seam and leaving a small gap in one edge for turning. Trim seam and across corners, turn board right side out and slip stitch gap in seam.

Press board lightly, then machine-stitch along all the lines of braid. Now sew braid around the outer edge. Stitch a 2cm (¾in) square of hooked Velcro strip to the centre of each square.

To make the noughts

Place two pieces of printed fabric with right sides together and put them on top of a layer of wadding. Place the paper nought pattern on top of the fabric and pin it to all layers. Stitch all round close to the edge of the pattern. Now mark the dots onto fabric by pushing a pencil point through pattern at each dot into the fabric. Remove pattern and cut out the circle 3mm (⅛in) away from the stitching line.

Join up the dots with pencil lines, as shown on the pattern. Pull the two layers of fabric apart and cut along the two marked lines in one layer of fabric only.

Turn the nought right side out carefully through the slits, then stuff lightly. Sew a 2cm (¾in) square of furry Velcro strip to centre of nought, to cover the slits.

To make the crosses

Make exactly as for the noughts, using the cross pattern.

PUMPKIN PINCUSHIONS

You won't believe how quickly these squashy fruits can be produced! They measure 9cm (3½in) across and their effectiveness depends on the choice of fabric – striped cotton seersucker, which gives them that pumpkin-like ridged look. The leaf is handy for holding needles which tend to disappear right inside pincushions, but for extra speed you could omit the leaf and just make the stalk.

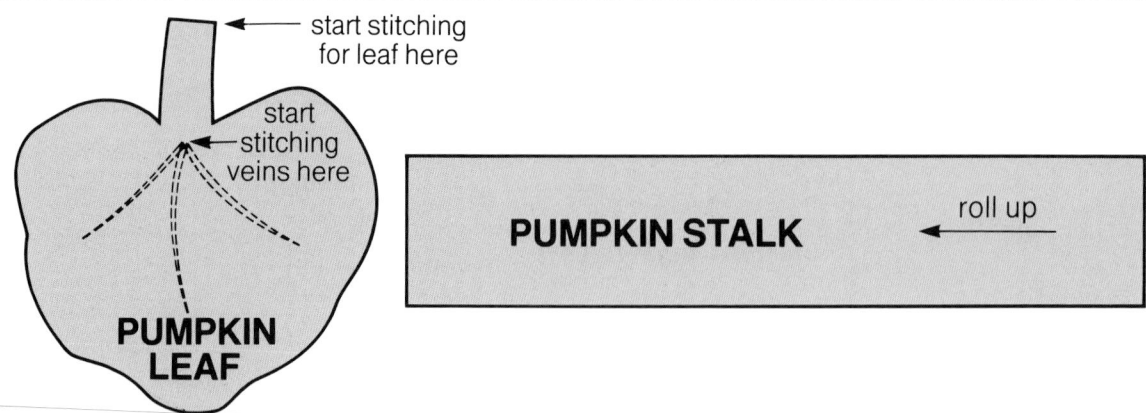

start stitching for leaf here

start stitching veins here

PUMPKIN LEAF

PUMPKIN STALK

roll up

You will need: Small pieces of yellow or green seersucker fabric and green felt; stuffing.

Notes: Trace leaf and stalk patterns onto thin paper and cut out. Seams are as stated in the instructions.

To make

Cut a 12×28cm (4¾×11in) strip of fabric, noting that seersucker stripes should run parallel with short edges of strip.

Join short edges, taking a 5mm (¼in) seam and leave wrong side out. Gather round, 5mm (¼in) away from one of the remaining raw edges, pull up gathers tightly and fasten off securely. Turn right side out and stuff. Gather round the remaining raw edge as before, pull up gathers, turning raw edges to inside, then fasten off but do not break thread.

Take needle through centre of pumpkin from one gathered edge to the other, then back again. Pull thread tightly to make squat shape, then fasten off.

Cut the stalk from felt and roll it up tightly along the length, then sew short end in place. Sew one end to gathered top of pumpkin. Pin the paper-leaf pattern to two layers of felt, then stitch all round close to edge of pattern. Knot thread ends. Remove pattern and cut out leaf close to stitching line.

Starting at point indicated on pattern, stitch up and down each vein line in turn. Draw thread ends through to one side of leaf and knot, then sew them between layers of felt. Sew short end of leaf to the stalk.

BOBBLE DOLLS

These appealing little dolls measure 17cm (6¾in) from the tops of their bobble caps to their toes. You can stitch them as toys just to play with, or add two to the ends of a scarf. The dolls also have their own little scarves, which are removable.

They are easy and economical to make using simple rectangular shapes cut from stretch towelling – the kind sold for making track-suits or sweat shirts.

You will need: 25cm (10in) of 152cm (60in) wide striped stretch towelling (this is enough to make one scarf and several dolls); small piece of pale pink stretch towelling; small amount of washable stuffing; lengths of black double knitting yarn and red thread; red pencil.

Notes: The patterns for the dolls are printed full-size. Take care to cut out all the pieces, having the arrows marked on each pattern going across the *width* of the fabric. Stretch towelling stretches the most across the width and you need to cut the pieces correctly in order to make a plump little doll.

Seams measuring 3mm (⅛in) are allowed on the doll pieces and 5mm (¼in) seams on the full-size scarf. Join all the pieces right sides together unless otherwise stated. When making the doll, use the smooth (wrong) side of the pink towelling as the *right* side for the head and hands. Stuff the doll softly and evenly so that the towelling stretches slightly.

Since stretch towelling is a knitted type of fabric, it is quite often sold tube-shaped with folds at each side and no cut selvedges. If your towelling is like this, cut it open at one fold before making a start. To ensure that

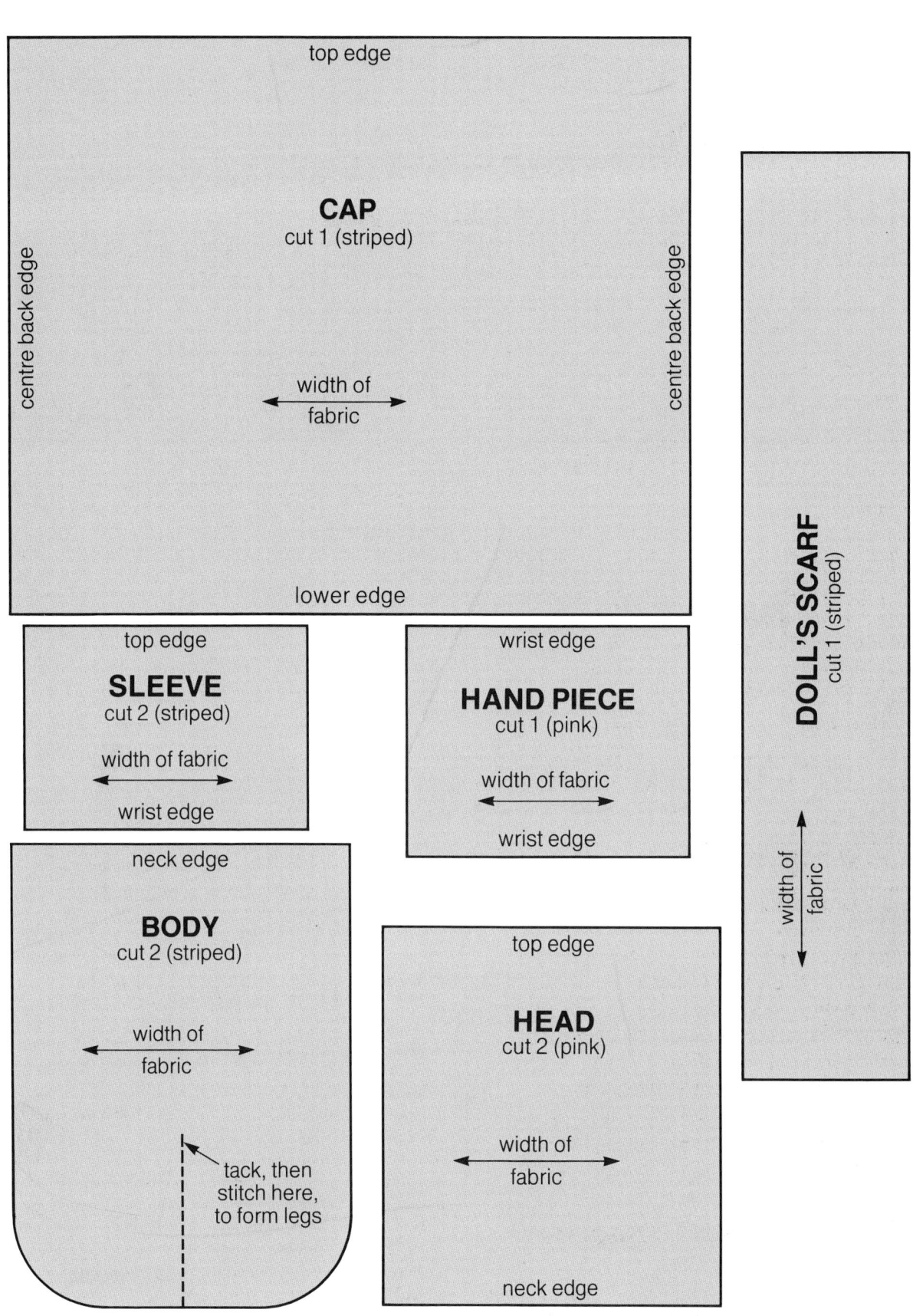

the stripes match when making the body and arm pieces, cut these one at a time, placing one edge of the pattern level with a stripe and doing the same for the matching piece. If you cut from double fabric, it is unlikely that the stripes will match.

To ensure accurate seaming, tack all the pieces loosely together as you go. The scarf strip is cut across the entire width of the fabric, so if making the scarf, cut this strip *first*, then make the dolls from the left-over remnants.

To make the scarf

Cut a 15cm (6in) strip across the 152cm (60in) width of the fabric, following the stripes. Bring the short raw edges together and join the long side edges to within 10cm (4in) of the ends, leaving a small gap in one seam for turning. Now continue stitching the seams at the long edges, tapering each to a point at the centre of each short edge. You can see this clearly in the colour photograph. Trim off the excess fabric at the tapered ends, then turn the scarf right side out and slip stitch the gap.

To make the doll

Cut two body pieces from striped fabric and two head pieces from pink fabric. Join the neck edges of body pieces to neck edges of head pieces.

Now join the complete pieces to each other, leaving the top edges of the head open. Turn right side out. To form the legs, tack, then stitch through the centre of body, as shown on the pattern. Pull sewing threads through to one side of fabric, knot them, then sew into body between the fabric layers.

Stuff each leg, then body and head. Run a gathering thread around the top of the head, pull up tightly, turning in raw edges, then fasten off securely. Run a doubled gathering thread around head just above neck seam, pull up gathers to shape the neck, then fasten off.

Cut one hand piece from pink fabric. Note that only *one* piece is required because a length of sewing thread is tied around at the centre later on, to give the effect of *two* hands.

Cut two sleeve pieces from striped fabric. Join the wrist edge of one sleeve to one wrist edge of the hand piece. Repeat with the other sleeve. Now join the long edges of this completed hand and sleeve piece. Turn right side out and stuff. Turn in the top raw edge of each sleeve and oversew to close completely.

Tie sewing thread tightly round at the centre of the hand piece, thus making two hands. Knot threads securely, then sew thread ends into hands. Sew top edges of sleeves to side seams of body, just below the neck, as shown in the photograph.

Mark the position of the eyes with pins 2.5cm (1in) up from neck, spacing them 1.5cm (⅝in) apart. Before removing the pins, mark the positions with a pencil. Thread a needle with a length of black yarn and knot one end. Take needle through from back of head (where it will be hidden by cap) to marked position of one eye. Take needle back through head again, a little above marked point to make a tiny vertical stitch. Fasten off yarn. Repeat for the other eye.

Use double red thread to work a small horizontal stitch in the same way, 1cm (⅜in) below eyes. Colour cheeks and mark a dot for nose, using a red pencil.

Cut one cap piece from striped fabric and join centre back edges. Turn 1cm (⅛in) at lower edge to wrong side and tack loosely. Leaving cap wrong side out, gather around top edge. If making the doll only, pull up the gathers tightly and fasten off. If attaching doll to scarf, push one pointed end of scarf inside lower edge of cap, then pull the point through until it protrudes slightly above the gathered edge of cap. Pull up gathers tightly around the scarf point, then fasten off. Sew gathers securely to point of scarf.

Now turn the cap right side out and push a small ball of stuffing in the top. Gather around cap just below stuffing, pull up tightly and fasten off, thus forming the bobble.

Place cap on doll's head with seam at the centre

back, having it just above eyes at front and slightly lower at back. Slip stitch lower edge of cap to head.

Cut one doll's scarf piece from striped fabric. Join the long edges and across one short edge. Turn right side out, using the knob of a knitting-needle. Turn in the remaining raw edge, and slip stitch to close. Wind a length of sewing thread tightly around, 1cm (⅜in) away from each end of scarf to form bobbles. Knot threads and sew ends into scarf. Tie scarf around doll's neck.

SLEEPY PUPPIES

These endearing dozy doggies should be full of beans because they are filled with lentils. Each measures about 10cm (4in) from their front paws to tip of their tails and for extra play value you can make a little slipper, 11cm (4¼in) in length, for the puppy to sleep in.

For each puppy you will need: Scraps of fawn fleecy fabric, ribbon, black felt and white felt; black thread; 28g (1oz) of lentils; brown permanent marker pen.

For the slipper you will need: Scraps of tweedy fabric, ribbon, felt, thin card and iron-on interfacing; adhesive.

Notes: All the patterns are given full-size for tracing off the page. For the puppy body and slipper sole the patterns are *halved* because it is easier to trace off and cut out these shapes from folded paper.

Place fold in paper to the edge indicated on each pattern, trace off, cut out, then open up to give the complete pattern.

You can leave the puppy plain fawn, or mark the fabric with a pen to get a patched effect, like the puppies illustrated. Seams are as stated in the instructions.

THE PUPPY

The body

Pin the body pattern to two layers of fleecy fabric, having right sides of fabric together. Machine-stitch all around the body, close to the edge of the pattern, leaving a gap in the stitching at the back of the body as shown on the pattern.

Before removing the pattern, trim fabric 3mm (⅛in) away from the pattern at the gap in the stitching.

Remove the pattern and cut out the body close to the stitching line. Turn right side out, using the knob end of a knitting-needle to turn the front paws first, then the back paws. Fill the body with lentils, then ladder stitch the gap in the seam.

Now mark the body lightly here and there with a pen, blotting the marks with a paper tissue as you make them to press the colour into the fabric. Leave until dry before handling again.

In one of the layers of body fabric, ladder stitch a dart along the length of the body, as shown on the pattern. You don't have to be too precise about this – it is only done to make the underbody a bit smaller than the upper body.

Use double black thread to make three stitches around the end of each paw as follows. Take your needle through one leg and bring it out at the position of the centre stitch, underneath the paw. Do not pull the thread right through, leave the ends sticking out of the leg. Now work a tiny back stitch where the needle came out, then tug to see if the thread is secure. If the thread comes through, start again and work two back stitches this time. When the thread is secured, you can work all the paw stitches, taking the thread through the leg to each stitch position. Fasten off as you started, then take the needle back through the leg again. Pull the thread ends and snip them off close to the leg. The cut ends will disappear into the leg.

The head

Stitch the head in same way as for the body, leaving a gap in stitching as shown on the pattern. Cut out, etc as for the body. Turn the head right side out and fill with lentils, then ladder stitch gap. Colour with pen to match body.

Cut two eye pieces from white felt and two smaller pupils from black felt, as shown on the head pattern. Glue them together in pairs as shown on pattern. You can experiment with the eyes by gluing on the pupils in different positions to make your puppy glance sideways or downwards instead of upwards. Glue the eyes to head as shown on the pattern. Cut nose from black felt

and glue in place as shown. Do not sew head to body just yet.

The ears

Cut one pair of ears from fleecy fabric. Turn in all the raw edges a fraction and catch them down, slip stitching the edges in place. Colour ears as for body. Sew tops of ears to head as shown on the head pattern, having the inner edges of ears nearest to the puppy's eyes. Catch ears to head underneath, just above lower pointed ends.

The tail

Cut tail from fleecy fabric and oversew side edges neatly together, having right side of fabric outside. Sew open end of tail to back of body.

To assemble head and body

Place back of head upon front of body with chin resting just onto front legs. Turn the head slightly either to right or left, depending on which way you want your puppy to face. Pin back of head to body where they touch, to keep in position. Now ladder stitch head to body, working a small circle of stitches at the pinned position. Tie a ribbon bow around the puppy's neck (the ladder-stitched circle).

With your puppy's head facing towards you, bring the back leg which is furthest away from you against the body. Pin in place, then ladder stitch it to the body.

THE SLIPPER

Cut the slipper sole from thin card, then cut another one or two if your card is very thin and glue them all together. Mark points A and B on the card sole. Cut a sole piece from felt and glue it to the unmarked side of the card. This felt-covered side will be on the inside of the slipper.

Iron the interfacing onto wrong side of your piece of slipper fabric. Cut one pair of slipper uppers and join them at the centre front edges, taking a 5mm (¼in) seam. Press the seam open with your fingers, then glue the seam allowance flat.

Turn in the top edge of slipper 5mm (¼in) and glue it down, clipping the fabric at curves if necessary, to make it turn. Join the centre back edges in the same way as for the front, gluing down the seam allowance. Turn slipper right side out.

Place slipper sole inside the lower edge of slipper, having the felt-covered side of card on the inside of slipper and matching points A and B on both. Turn 5mm (¼in) of the lower edge of slipper on to card sole and glue in place, easing slipper fabric to fit.

Now cut another card sole and glue it under slipper to cover the raw edges of fabric. Sew a small ribbon bow to front of slipper.

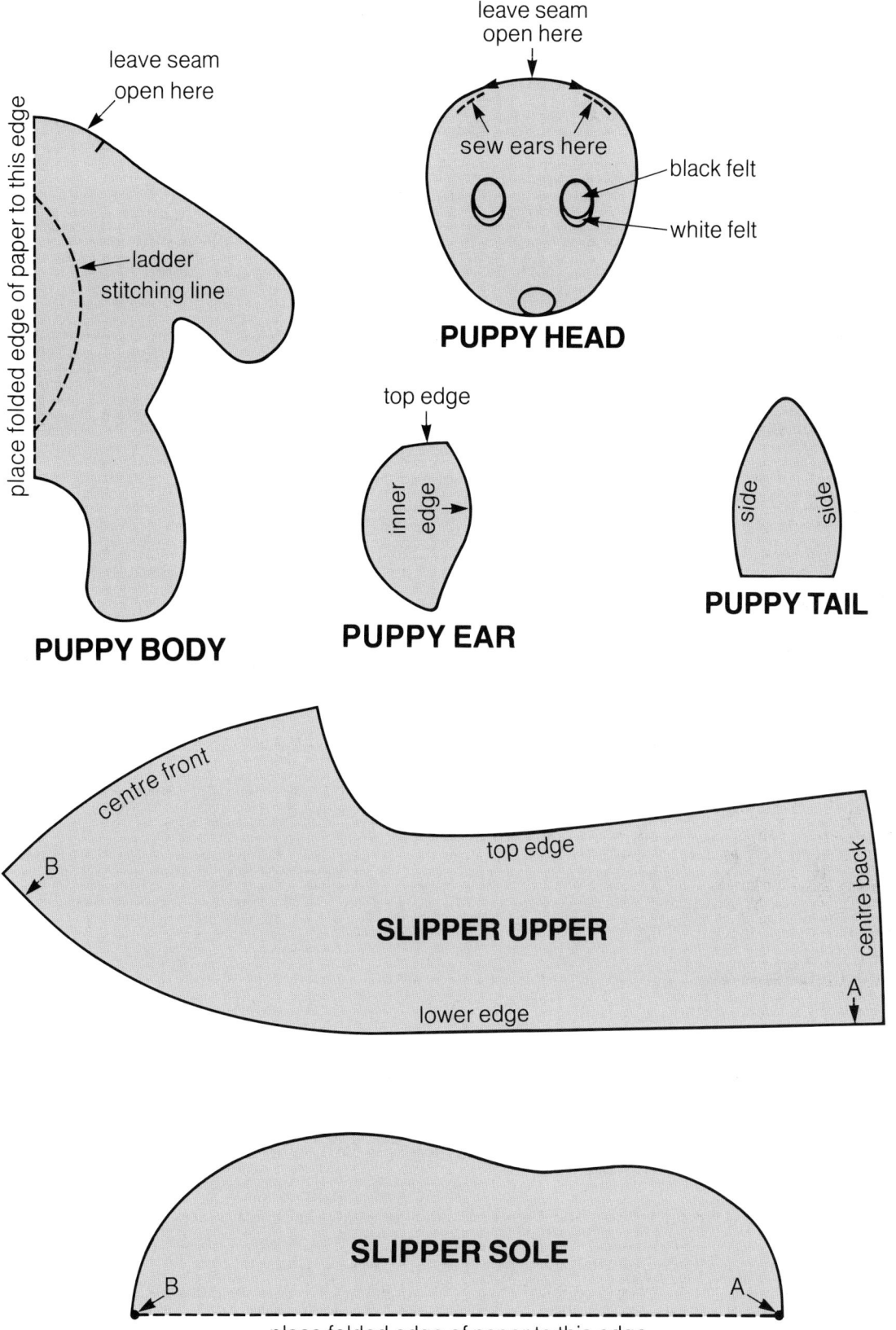

leave seam open here

place folded edge of paper to this edge

ladder stitching line

PUPPY BODY

leave seam open here

sew ears here

black felt

white felt

PUPPY HEAD

top edge

inner edge

PUPPY EAR

side

side

PUPPY TAIL

centre front

B

top edge

SLIPPER UPPER

centre back

A

lower edge

B

SLIPPER SOLE

A

place folded edge of paper to this edge

PENCIL-CASE

Here is a novelty pencil-case measuring 9 × 21cm (3½ × 8¼in), in the shape of a parcel which is very quick and easy to make. You can add the fabric label then leave it blank, so that the child can fill in his or her name and form number.

You will need: Small pieces of fabric; 80cm (⅞yd) of narrow ribbon; a 20cm (8in) zip fastener.

Note: Seams are as stated in the instructions.

To make

Cut two 11 × 23cm (4¼ × 9in) pieces of fabric. If you are using thin fabric such as gingham, cut two more pieces for lining. Tack lining pieces to pencil-case pieces.

Sew ribbon strips to right side of each case piece, as shown in the colour photograph, stitching down the centre of ribbon.

For the label, cut a 4.5 × 7cm (1¾ × 2¾in) piece of white fabric. Turn in raw edges 1cm (⅜in) and press. Sew label to one corner of one case piece. Make small ribbon bow and sew to case where strips of ribbon cross over.

Turn in and press 1cm (⅜in) at top edges of each case piece. Stitch these edges to tapes on either side of the zip. Open up the zip.

Fold the case, right sides together. Join pieces along lower and side edges, taking a 1cm (⅜in) seam. Trim off corners and ends of zip tapes, then turn case right side out through the zip.

FABRIC BEAD NECKLACES

Pick some scraps of finely woven fabric with small delicate patterns to create a stunningly simple necklace or two. Add a few glass or plastic beads if you have them, but for real economy cut a bamboo garden cane into small sections and use these instead. As well as being cheap, the bamboo beads add an ethnic, hand-made touch (see also p. 113).

I used Liberty lawn fabric for the beads illustrated in the colour photo-graph, the one red and two black beads being made from precious scraps which I had saved for over twenty years! Each bead is about 2.5cm (1in) in length and you can thread them onto a shoe-lace or a length of Russian braid.

You will need: Oddments of thin soft fabrics and stuffing; four glass or plastic beads with large holes (or four 1cm (⅜in) long sections cut off a bamboo garden cane); one bead with a large hole for necklace fastening; 50cm (20in) of narrow braid such as Russian braid, or length of shoe-lace; a pair of tweezers and pliers; a thick bodkin.

Note: Seams are as stated in the instructions.

To make the beads

For each bead (you will need three), cut a 4×7cm (1½×2¾in) strip of fabric. Join the short edges of strip, taking a 3mm (⅛in) seam.

Keeping wrong side out, gather around 3mm (⅛in) away from one raw edge. Place bodkin inside gathered edge, then pull up gathers tightly around bodkin and fasten off securely. This is done so as to leave a hole for threading. Remove the bodkin and turn fabric right side out.

Stuff firmly, using tweezers to push in the stuffing. Gather the remaining raw edge around bodkin as before, pushing the raw edge to the inside with tweezers before fastening off securely.

To thread the beads

Thread on the fabric beads and the other beads alternately as shown in the photograph. Thread the fabric beads as follows. Using the bodkin threaded with a shoe-lace or narrow braid, push the bodkin through holes at each end of bead. Now use pliers to pull bodkin right through. If you find that the gathered raw edges pull through to the outside when doing this, push them back inside with the tweezers.

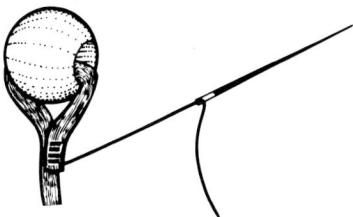

DIAGRAM, showing how to sew on bead for the fastening

To make the fastening

Thread the ordinary bead onto one end of braid or shoe-lace. Loop the end around bead, then sew to hold bead in place as shown in the diagram. To neaten this join, wind sewing thread tightly around and around the end of the braid and the sewn portion, then sew thread end into wound portion.

Make a loop at the other end of the braid in the same way, just large enough to fit over the bead.

the box surfaces, except for the top of the box which has the opening in it. Glue them all in place, taking care to cut a hole in the particular reinforcing card piece for the winding screw to pass through.

Pack the inside of the box with crumpled paper (newspaper will do), then cut a piece of card to fit top of box and glue it in place.

Cut a piece of white fleecy fabric to fit top of box and glue it in place. Cover underneath base of box in same way, using felt.

Cut a 5cm (2in) wide strip of fabric to go all around the sides of the box. Glue in place, starting at one corner and cutting a hole in the fabric for the winding screw to pass through. You can now screw the winding key back in place.

Glue the lengths of braid around the sides of the box level with the edges of top and base of box, as shown in the photograph.

THE SLEIGH

Cut the sleigh base from corrugated reinforced card to the size of the dotted line on pattern, having corrugations going *across* the card as shown on pattern. Cut a piece of yellow felt to the size of the solid outline of pattern. Glue the card to the felt as shown on pattern. Turn narrow edges of felt over to other side of card base and glue them in place. Turn the larger piece of felt over to the other side of card and glue in place also. Having the side of card which is completely covered with felt uppermost, bend up the front edge of the sleigh in a smooth curve, then lay it aside for now.

Cut two sleigh side pieces from reinforced card and glue them to pieces of felt, taking care to reverse one card piece when doing this, to make a *pair*. Cut out the felt 1cm (⅜in) larger than the card all around the edges. Clip this extra felt at the curves and trim at the corners. Turn and stick the extra felt to the other side of the card.

Now assemble sleigh pieces. Place sides of sleigh against long edges of base, having felt-covered surfaces of side pieces facing each other, so they will be on the inside of the sleigh. Take care to have curled up portion of base following the curve at lower edge of side pieces. Oversew lower edges of sleigh sides to long edges of base.

For the harness, cut two 14cm (5½in) lengths of shoe-lace and glue one end of each to the outsides of the sleigh at the position shown on side piece pattern.

To cover the remaining card surfaces of the sleigh

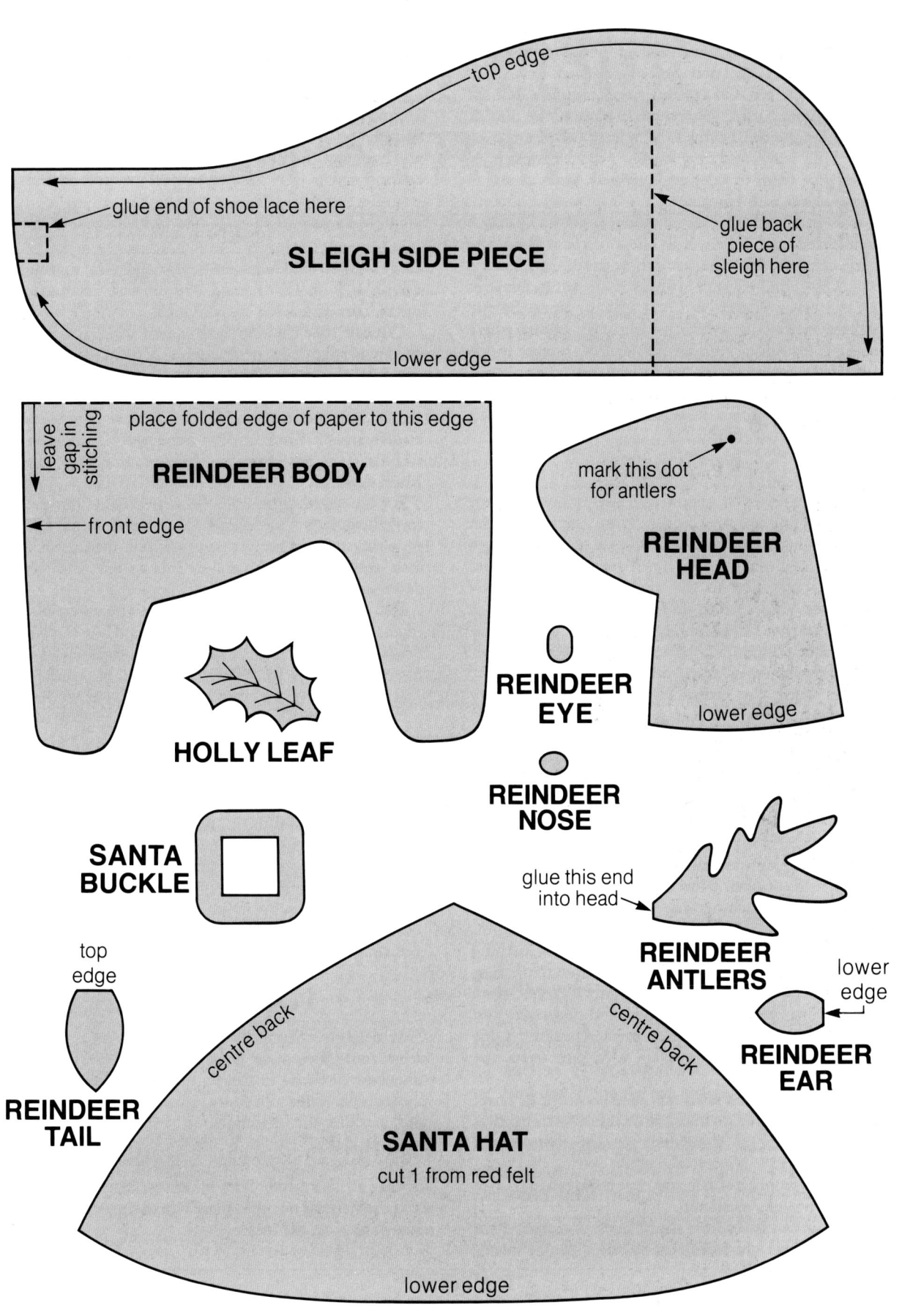

top edge

glue end of shoe lace here

SLEIGH SIDE PIECE

glue back piece of sleigh here

lower edge

leave gap in stitching

place folded edge of paper to this edge

REINDEER BODY

front edge

mark this dot for antlers

REINDEER HEAD

lower edge

HOLLY LEAF

REINDEER EYE

REINDEER NOSE

SANTA BUCKLE

glue this end into head

REINDEER ANTLERS

lower edge

REINDEER EAR

top edge

centre back

centre back

REINDEER TAIL

SANTA HAT
cut 1 from red felt

lower edge

You will need: Scraps of fabric and firm iron-on interfacing; thin card; stuffing; adhesive.

Notes: 5mm (¼in) seams are allowed on the segmented ball design. The pentagon pieces are oversewn together at the edges. All patterns are printed full-size.

To make the segmented ball

Use the pattern to cut four pieces from one printed fabric, then four from another. Now join two of these different fabric pieces at one long curved edge. Continue joining on pieces at one long edge, alternating the fabrics. Before joining the two final edges to complete the ball, machine-stitch twice along the short end edges to prevent stretching when the ball is stuffed. Now join the final two long edges.

Turn the ball right side out through one end. Stuff carefully, pushing in a little stuffing at a time and working through each open end. Use the end of a pencil to push stuffing right inside. Continue until ball is filled and nicely rounded.

Cut two end circles from interfacing and iron them onto wrong side of another printed fabric. Cut out the fabric about 1cm (⅜in) larger all round than the interfacing. Turn this surplus fabric over to the other side of the interfacing and tack.

Pin a circle centrally over each open end of the ball and slip stitch it in place. Remove the tacking threads.

The seams on the ball can be ironed if necessary, using a steam iron or hot iron over a damp cloth.

To make the pentagon ball

Trace off and cut out, then glue the pentagon shape to

a piece of thin card. Use this template to draw round, onto the interfacing. Draw, then cut twelve of these shapes from the interfacing. Iron them onto wrong side of bits of fabric. Cut out the fabrics about 1cm (⅜in) larger all round than the interfacing shapes.

Fold this surplus fabric to other side of interfacing shape at each edge in turn, tacking as you go. You must make sure that the fabric is exactly level with the edges of the interfacing when doing this, so that the finished shapes will fit perfectly together.

Lay out one shape and place five of the others around it as shown in the diagram. When you are

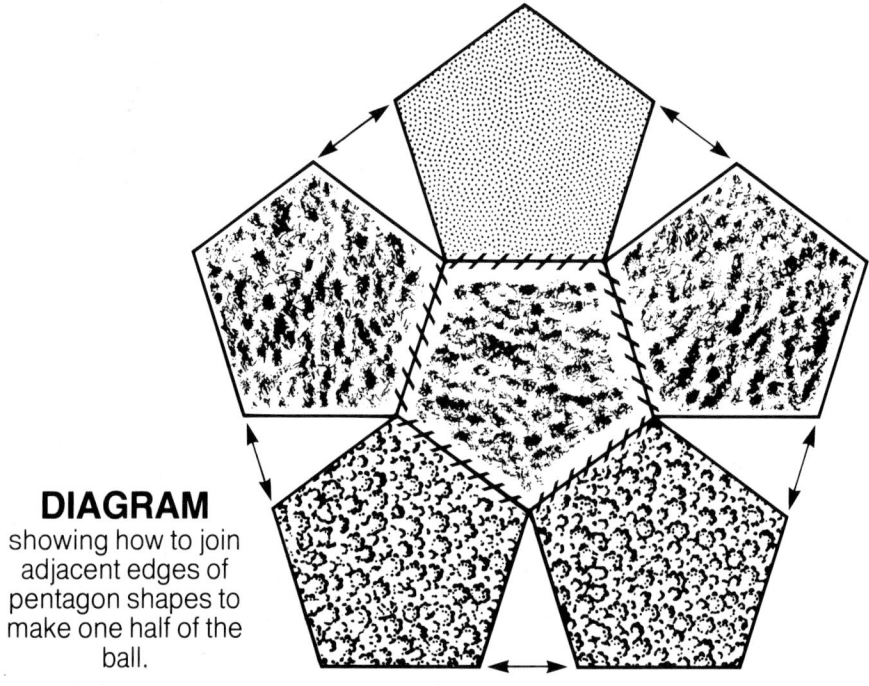

DIAGRAM
showing how to join adjacent edges of pentagon shapes to make one half of the ball.

pleased with the arrangement of the different patterned pieces, join them to the edges of the centre shape as follows.

Place the centre shape and one of the other shapes with right side together and all edges level. Oversew one pair of edges together, fastening off securely at each end. Join the other four shapes to the remaining four edges of centre shape in same way.

Now join the adjacent edges of the five outer shapes, as shown by the arrows in the diagram. This completes one half of the ball. Make the other half, using the remaining six shapes, in the same way.

Having both shapes wrong side out, fit them into each other – the pointed edges of one will fit into the V-shaped edges of the other. Join these edges by oversewing as before, leaving the last pair of edges open for turning.

Turn ball right side out and stuff, then oversew the remaining edges neatly together. Remove all the tacking threads.

JUNIOR SHOULDER-BAGS

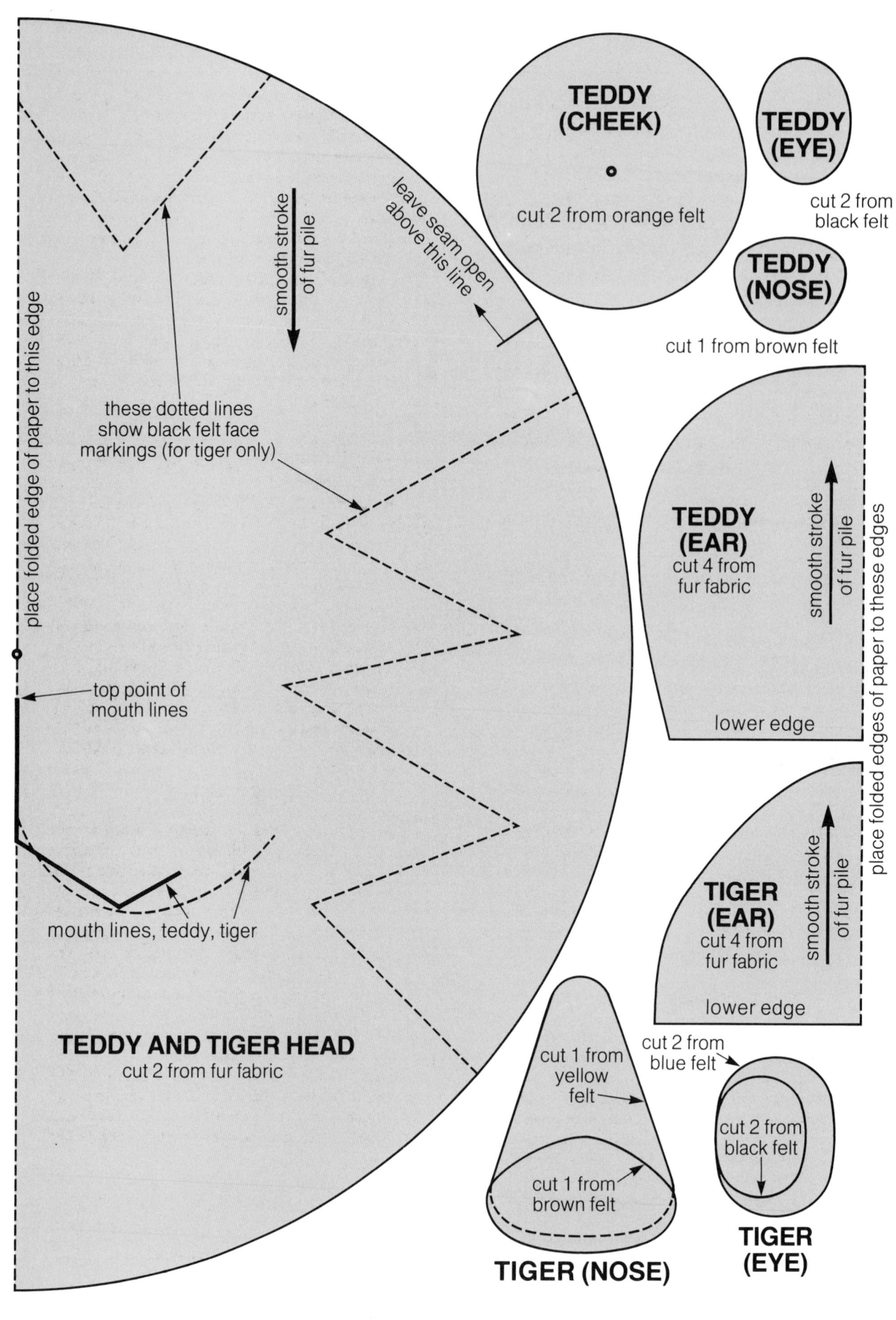

place folded edge of paper to this edge

smooth stroke of fur pile

leave seam open above this line

these dotted lines show black felt face markings (for tiger only)

top point of mouth lines

mouth lines, teddy, tiger

TEDDY AND TIGER HEAD
cut 2 from fur fabric

TEDDY (CHEEK)
cut 2 from orange felt

TEDDY (EYE)
cut 2 from black felt

TEDDY (NOSE)
cut 1 from brown felt

TEDDY (EAR)
cut 4 from fur fabric

smooth stroke of fur pile

lower edge

place folded edges of paper to these edges

TIGER (EAR)
cut 4 from fur fabric

smooth stroke of fur pile

lower edge

cut 1 from yellow felt

cut 1 from brown felt

cut 2 from blue felt

cut 2 from black felt

TIGER (NOSE)

TIGER (EYE)

They're cuddly, fun and easy to sew – a pair of shoulder-bags for the children, made from fur fabric and bits of felt. For extra strength, you can add an inner lining (using bits of ordinary fabric from the rag-bag), although this is not essential. Each bag measures about 22cm (8¾in) across.

If you need to buy fur fabric, the most economical way is to purchase 25cm (⅜yd) of 138cm (54in) wide and this will make two bags. Cut four bag circles first, then cut the straps from the remaining piece, joining them as necessary to make the required length.

You will need: Oddments of yellow or orange fur fabric (or purchase the amount mentioned); scraps of black, blue, yellow, orange and brown felt; oddments of ordinary woven fabric for lining; 3 large snap fasteners; black thread.

Notes: All the patterns can be traced off the page. The main bag piece (head), and the teddy and tiger ear patterns should be traced onto folded paper, placing the folded edge to dotted line indicated on each pattern. Cut them out folded, then open up to give the complete pattern. Mark the mouth lines on both halves of the head pattern. The patterns for tiger's eye and nose pieces overlay each other to show how they are assembled. The tiger face markings are printed in this way also, overlaying the head.

When cutting out, take care to have the smooth stroke of fur pile in direction shown on each pattern. Seams are as stated in the instructions. Sew all the felt pieces and ears in place by hand.

TEDDY BEAR BAG

Cut two head pieces from yellow fur fabric. Keeping pattern pinned to wrong side of one piece, mark on the teddy mouth line by pushing a pencil point through the pattern and into the fabric at intervals. Remove pattern and join up the dots. Using black thread and having wrong side of fabric uppermost, machine-stitch several times along the marked lines, starting and ending stitching at top point shown on pattern. Cut teddy nose, eye and cheek pieces from felt, as stated on patterns.

Sew nose to face, just lapping it over top point of mouth line. Sew eyes on either side, then sew cheeks in place, as shown in the colour photograph (p. 93).

Cut four teddy ears from yellow fur fabric. Oversew them together in pairs around the curved edges, leaving lower edges open. Turn right side out and oversew the lower edges of each one together. Pin the lower edges to face above eyes, 3cm (1¼in) within the raw edge of face and placing them 8cm (3in) apart. Sew the lower edges in place as pinned.

Now join the head pieces around the edges, taking a 1cm (⅜in) seam, leaving seam open above the line indicated on pattern and taking care not to catch ears in seam. Leaving the head wrong side out, turn down 1cm (⅜in) at these raw edges and slip stitch in place. Turn head right side out, then catch back of ears to outer edge of head piece to hold them in upright position.

For the shoulder strap, cut a 7×58cm (2¾×23in) strip of yellow fur fabric (or join shorter strips to make this length). Note that the length can be adjusted to suit the size of child. Join the long edges of strip, right side inside, and taking a 1cm (⅜in) seam. Oversew across one short end, then use the knob of a knitting-needle to push this end through and turn strap right side out. Sew ends of strap to inside of bag at each side of the opening, behind the ears.

If you wish to line the bag, cut two head pieces and seam them together, leaving an opening as for the fur fabric circles, but take a 1.5cm (⅝in) seam. Turn in 1.5cm (⅝in) on the raw edges of opening and tack. Leave lining wrong side out and place it inside the bag. Slip stitch open edges of lining to open edges of bag. Sew three snap fasteners to opening on the inside.

TIGER BAG

Cut two head pieces from orange fur fabric. Trace the face marking pieces separately off the page, noting that the top piece should be traced onto folded paper. Cut one top and two side pieces from black felt. Sew these pieces to one head piece in positions shown on pattern.

Mark, then stitch mouth as for teddy. Cut eye pieces and pupils from felt as stated on patterns, then sew pupils to eyes as shown. Cut nose pieces and assemble in same way. Sew nose piece in place as for teddy. Sew eyes on either side of top of nose.

Join the head pieces, finish off edges of opening, and add shoulder strap as for teddy.

Make ears as for teddy, using orange fur fabric. Sew lower edges in place between the side and top face markings and 1cm (⅜in) within the outer edge of head.

Make lining and sew on snap fasteners as for teddy.

STRAWBERRY PINCUSHIONS

W*ho could resist these luscious fruits! They are a little larger than life-size and you can turn them out by the dozen from an oddment of red velvet and green felt for the stalks. I used a small sample of curtain velvet for the strawberries illustrated, but any red fabric or felt will do.*

You will need: Scraps of red velvet (or other fabric) and green felt; stuffing; black fine-tipped permanent marker pen; strong thread for gathering; adhesive.

Notes: The patterns are given full-size. Mark rows of seeds on the strawberry pattern. Seams are as stated in the instructions.

To make

Cut the strawberry from red fabric, placing the edge of the pattern indicated to fold in fabric. Open up folded strawberry. Replace pattern on right side of one half of strawberry and use pencil point to mark dots for seeds through the pattern and into fabric. Reverse pattern and repeat on the other half. Now mark each pencil dot with a black pen. Leave to dry.

Fold strawberry in half again and stitch a 3mm (⅛in) seam as shown on the pattern. Turn right side out and gather with strong thread around the top raw edge. Stuff strawberry, pull up gathers tightly and fasten off, but leave needle threaded.

Cut stalk from green felt. Roll it up tightly along the length around a darning needle. Glue or sew the short end in place, then remove needle. Catch one end of stalk to top of strawberry using the threaded needle.

Cut strawberry top from green felt, then snip tiny hole at the centre, as shown on the pattern. Thread it onto the stalk, then glue in place on gathered top of strawberry.

FAKE CAKES

These naughty but nice sweet temptations are just right for those who are weight-watching! I designed them as pop-art pincushions, using mostly bits of matt and shiny dress-lining fabric. All the cakes are about life-size.

yellow when used for the correct purpose, it colours fabric golden brown. These pens are widely available from retail outlets which supply materials to schools, colleges and technical drawing offices and they cost about the same as normal permanent marker pens.

Use strong thread when gathering the circles. Note that the main pieces of the pincushions are made from double thickness fabric, to strengthen them.

Pincushions should be really firmly stuffed. The card bases should not be visible through the fabric.

CHERRY-TOPPED ICED BUN

Cut a 14cm (5½in) diameter circle from double-thickness fawn fabric. Gather around the edge through both thicknesses. Pull up gathers slightly and stuff.

Cut a 7cm (2¾in) diameter circle of card. Place this inside the gathered edge of fabric. Pull up gathers so that fabric covers about 1.5cm (⅝in) of the card circle around the edge, leaving a 4cm (1½in) diameter circle of card exposed at the centre. Fasten off gathering thread. Use a warm iron to flatten gathers against card base. Sew a 6cm (2¼in) diameter circle of felt under bun to cover the raw edges of fabric.

For the icing, cut a 14cm (5½in) diameter circle of white fabric and one thin layer of wadding. Split wadding if necessary to get a really thin layer. Place circles together and gather around the edges. Pull up gathers until the raw edges just meet, having white fabric on outside, then fasten off. Flatten the circle, with gathers at centre. Place in position, gathered side down, on top of bun. Use pencil to lightly mark bun around the edge of the circle, then remove it and colour bun with a marker pen a little above and about 2cm (¾in) below the line. Now ladder stitch the icing to top of bun, working just underneath the turned in edge so that the stitches cannot be seen.

For the stick of angelica, cut a 4cm (1½in) diameter circle of green fabric. Fold it in half, then quarters, then

than card and sew it underneath eclair to cover edges.

Make icing in same way as for the iced bun, using an 8×12cm (3¼×4¾in) strip of dark brown fabric and of wadding, rounding them off at the short edges. Colour the bun, then sew icing in place as for the iced bun.

CREAM BUN

Make the top half of bun first, in same way as for the iced bun, using a 16cm (6¼in) diameter circle of double-thickness fawn fabric and a 7cm (2¾in) diameter circle of card. Felt circle can be omitted.

For the dusted icing effect, cut a 12cm (4¾in) diameter circle of net and a 6cm (2¼in) diameter circle of wadding, splitting the wadding to get the thinnest possible layer. Make as for the iced bun icing, then colour bun and sew icing in place in same way also.

For the bottom half of bun, cut an 8cm (3¼in) diameter circle of paper and pin it to two layers of fawn fabric, with a layer of wadding underneath. Stitch all round close to edge of paper, then remove pattern. Cut out circle close to stitching line. To turn right side out, pull apart the layers of fawn fabric, then cut a small slit in the centre of the outermost one. Turn right side out through slit, then stuff very lightly, keeping shape flat. Oversew edges of slit together, then colour all round edge of this circle. Note that you should keep this slit circle uppermost when sewing bun pieces together.

For the jam and the cream, cut a 6×12cm (2¼×4¾in) strip of red and one of white stockinette fabric. Place a little stuffing along length of each, then bring the long edges together, enclosing stuffing and having right side outside. Run a gathering thread all round edges of each. Gather slightly and fasten off.

Sew the jam, folded edge outwards to one side of the bun base. Sew cream on top of jam. Now place top of bun in position on top of base. Ladder stitch the two together where they touch. Ladder stitch top of bun to cream also, where it touches.

BOOT PENCIL·HOLDER

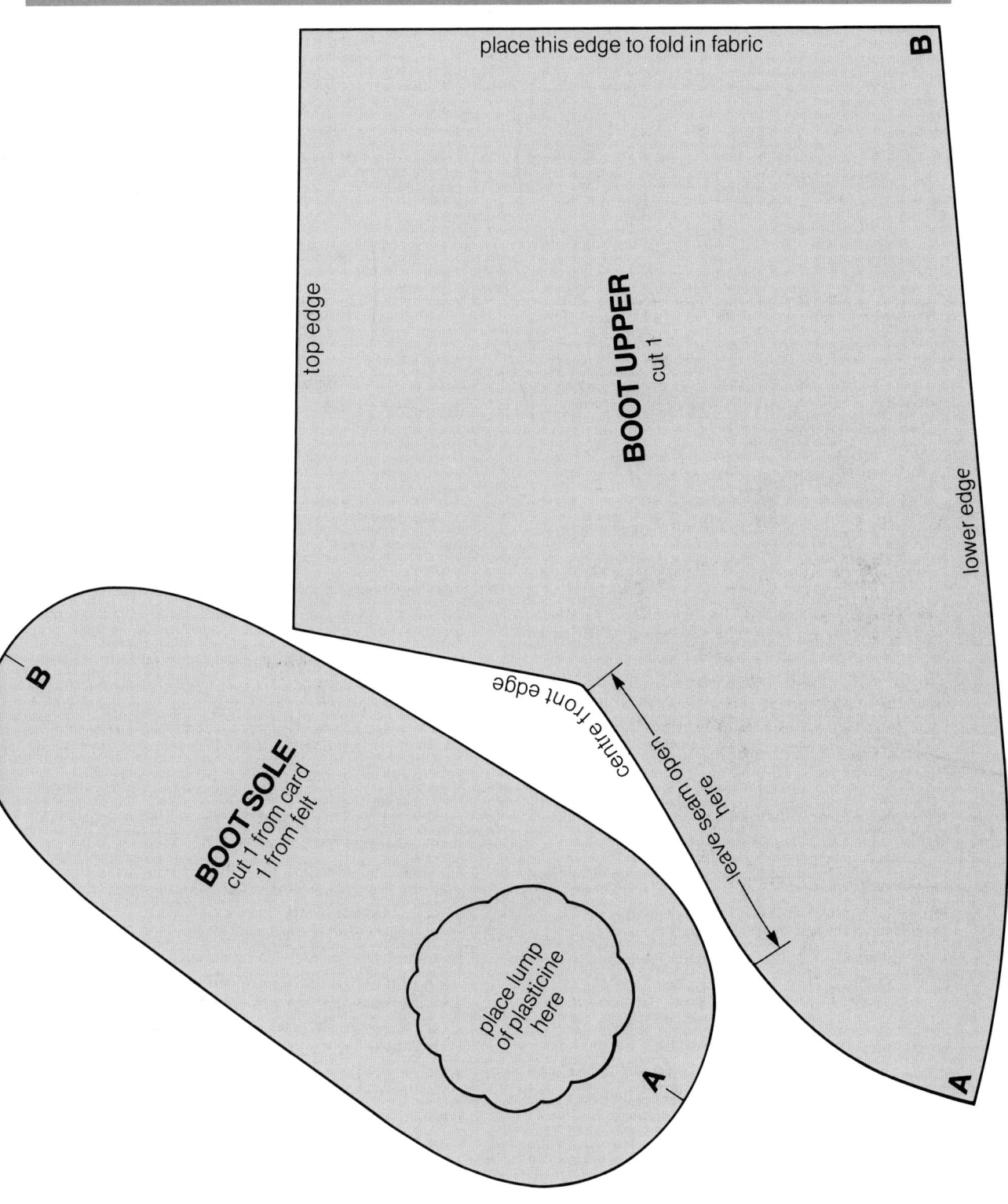

place this edge to fold in fabric

B

top edge

BOOT UPPER
cut 1

lower edge

centre front edge

leave seam open here

B

BOOT SOLE
cut 1 from card
1 from felt

place lump
of plasticine
here

A

A

stuffing; Plasticine; thin flexible card (about postcard weight); strong rigid card for the sole; small pieces of felt; adhesive.

Notes: The patterns are given full-size for tracing off the page. Seams are as stated in the instructions.

To make

Cut the boot upper, placing the edge of the pattern indicated to fold in fabric. Join the centre front edges, taking a 5mm (¼in) seam and leaving a gap in seam, as shown on pattern. Turn right side out.

Cut the sole from strong card and place it inside the lower raw edge of boot, matching points A and B. Glue the lower raw edges 1cm (⅜in) onto the sole all round. Put a lump of Plasticine about the size of a golf-ball inside the boot at position shown, then flatten it against the sole.

Cut a 10×40cm (4×16in) strip of thin card. Roll it up along the length and glue, to form a tube measuring about 18cm (7in) around. Place it inside the boot with one end resting against the sole.

Stuff the front of the boot through the gap in seam, then slip stitch gap. Glue the top raw edge of the boot to the top edge of the tube, pulling and stretching the fabric upwards away from the sole as you do this. Trim off any excess fabric which sticks up above the tube.

Glue a strip of shoe-lace around the lower edge of boot, level with the sole. Cut a sole from felt and stick it underneath boot to cover the raw edges of fabric.

Stick a strip of fancy braid down the centre front seam, turning in the corners at the end to form a point, as shown in the colour photograph. Glue fancy braid around top edge of boot, letting it extend slightly above the raw edge of fabric. Glue strip of shoe-lace around the inside, level with top edge of braid to cover top of tube and the raw edge of boot fabric.

A useful holder for a desk, or just to keep all those stray pens and pencils tidy around the house! The boot is about 10cm (4in) high and is inexpensive to make from bits and pieces.

You will need: Small piece of firm fabric such as quilted or foam-backed; 35cm (14in) length of fancy braid; 60cm (24in) length of 1cm (⅜in) wide sports-shoe-lace;

FUNNY FACES

These irresistible little characters can be made to delight the hearts of young and old alike. You only need scraps cut from nylon stockings or tights, tiny black beads and safety-pins, plus a few other readily available bits and pieces. Each brooch measures about 3cm (1¼in) across.

For the basic faces you will need: Cuttings off nylon tights or stockings (the plain-knit type are best and you can use light or dark shades, according to each character); a little stuffing; small piece of fawn felt to neaten the back of each brooch; tiny black seed beads (the kind which are used for Indian bead weaving); red, and pink or white beads about 4mm (³/₁₆in) in diameter for clown and grandmama's noses; small safety-pins; oddments of double knitting yarn (USA: worsted weight) in suitable 'hair' shades; fabric for head-scarf; scrap of yellow fur fabric for clown's hair; black and red thread; scraps of narrow ribbon, braid and lace edging; red,

blue and black pencils; thick black paper; adhesive.
Additional materials: For baby's soother: bit of flexible plastic, for example from a margarine tub lid, or washing up liquid bottle; for Indian: tiny feather; for grandmama's spectacles: medium fuse wire, a 4½mm (No 7, USA: 6) knitting-needle to bend the wire around and invisible nylon sewing thread for sewing in place.

Notes: Patterns are given full-size for tracing off the page. No seams required, only hand-sewing.

To make the basic face
Using the circular pattern, cut the head from a double thickness of nylon tights or stocking fabric. Gather around the circles through both thicknesses, near to the edges. Stuff circles firmly, then pull up gathers

tightly and fasten off. Gathers will be at the centre back of the head.

When working the facial features, have the knitted ribs in fabric going from top to bottom of face – you can see this clearly in the coloured photograph.

Mark positions of the eyes with pins first, placing them 1cm (⅜in) apart and half-way up face for the baby, a little higher up for the other characters. For grandmama, place pins a little higher up still and closer together. When you are satisfied with the positions, mark with a pencil.

To sew on each bead for the eye, use needle and double black thread. Secure thread at gathers, take needle through head to one marked position, thread on the bead, then pass needle back through at one side of the marked position. When you do this, have the hole in the bead horizontal (as shown in the diagram) to give the face a 'bright-eyed' look. Now pull thread tightly to depress bead into face, then fasten off. Repeat for other eye.

Work mouth stitches in same way, using red thread and working two stitches to form a V-shape. Omit the mouth on baby and refer to the photograph for size of stitches for the other faces.

Moisten red pencil lead slightly and mark a dot for nose on pirate, Indian, baby and girl with plaits. For the clown and grandmama, sew on the nose beads as for eyes, but do not pull thread tight. Colour cheeks lightly with red pencil, more heavily for clown. Now follow further instructions for each face.

Baby

To cut the soother, stick the circular paper pattern to bit of plastic, then cut out plastic level with paper, using sharp scissors. Peel off pattern. You can smooth off any corners or rough edges by rubbing edge of circle on a sandpaper-type of nail-file.

Cut the handle strip from plastic (you don't really need to use the pattern, just cut strip and compare to size shown on the page).

Pierce a small hole in the centre of circle and push both ends of handle through it. Let ends protrude about 3mm (⅛in) on other side of circle. To sew in place, take needle and double thread through from back of head as before, to position of mouth. Pass needle through protruding ends of handle, then take back through the head again. Pull thread tightly and fasten off.

Sew a tiny bunch of yarn strands on top of head, tease out ends, then trim if necessary.

Clown

Use black thread to work a small stitch beside and above each eye as shown in the colour photograph. Mark eyebrows above eyes using a blue pencil.

Cut the hair strip from fur fabric. Fold it in half with right side outside and oversew all raw edges together.

Sew this strip across top of head, from one side of face to the other, having folded edge of fabric above face.

Grandmama

Use black pencil to mark eyebrows above eyes. Sew a few loops of white yarn to forehead for hair. Bend the centre of a length of fuse wire half round a knitting-needle to form bridge of spectacles. On either side of this, wind wire twice around the needle to form lenses, then snip off ends of wire neatly.

Use nylon thread to sew spectacles in place, taking thread through from back of head as before. Sew bridge of spectacles above nose, then lower edges of lenses to cheeks.

Tie a bow at the centre of a bit of ribbon. Sew bow underneath chin. Take ends of ribbon up sides of face and sew there. Sew a piece of lacy edging across top of head for bonnet, lapping ends over ends of ribbon.

Girl with plaits

Cut six 20cm (8in) lengths of yarn. Sew centres to top of head, then catch strands together at each side of face. Plait the strands and tie around sewing thread to secure. Tease out ends of yarn, then trim them evenly. Tie ribbon bows around ends of plaits and sew through bows at centres to prevent them coming undone. Catch yarn strands to head here and there with tiny stitches, using matching sewing thread.

Pirate

Sew a few tiny yarn loops to top of head at one side for hair. Using pattern, cut eye patch from thick black paper (or colour a piece of paper black). Glue it in place over one eye. For the eye-patch strap, sew a strand of black thread around head, from one corner of eye-patch to the other, securing thread at back of head.

Cut the head-scarf from fabric. Turn in front and back edges 3mm (⅛in) and glue down. Wrap scarf around head, as shown in the colour photograph, bringing pointed ends together at side of head. Sew to head just above points as shown, so that points hang down. Arrange remainder of scarf in folds at back of head, then sew folds in place.

Indian

Make hair as for girl with plaits but use 12cm (4¾in) lengths of yarn and do not plait them.

Sew a strip of narrow braid around head, joining ends at back. Tuck feather into band at back and sew in place.

To finish off each brooch

Cut the felt circle and sew on the safety-pin, as shown on the pattern. Slip stitch edge of felt circle to back of brooch to cover gathers and stitches, taking care to have safety-pin positioned horizontally and nearest to the top of the head.

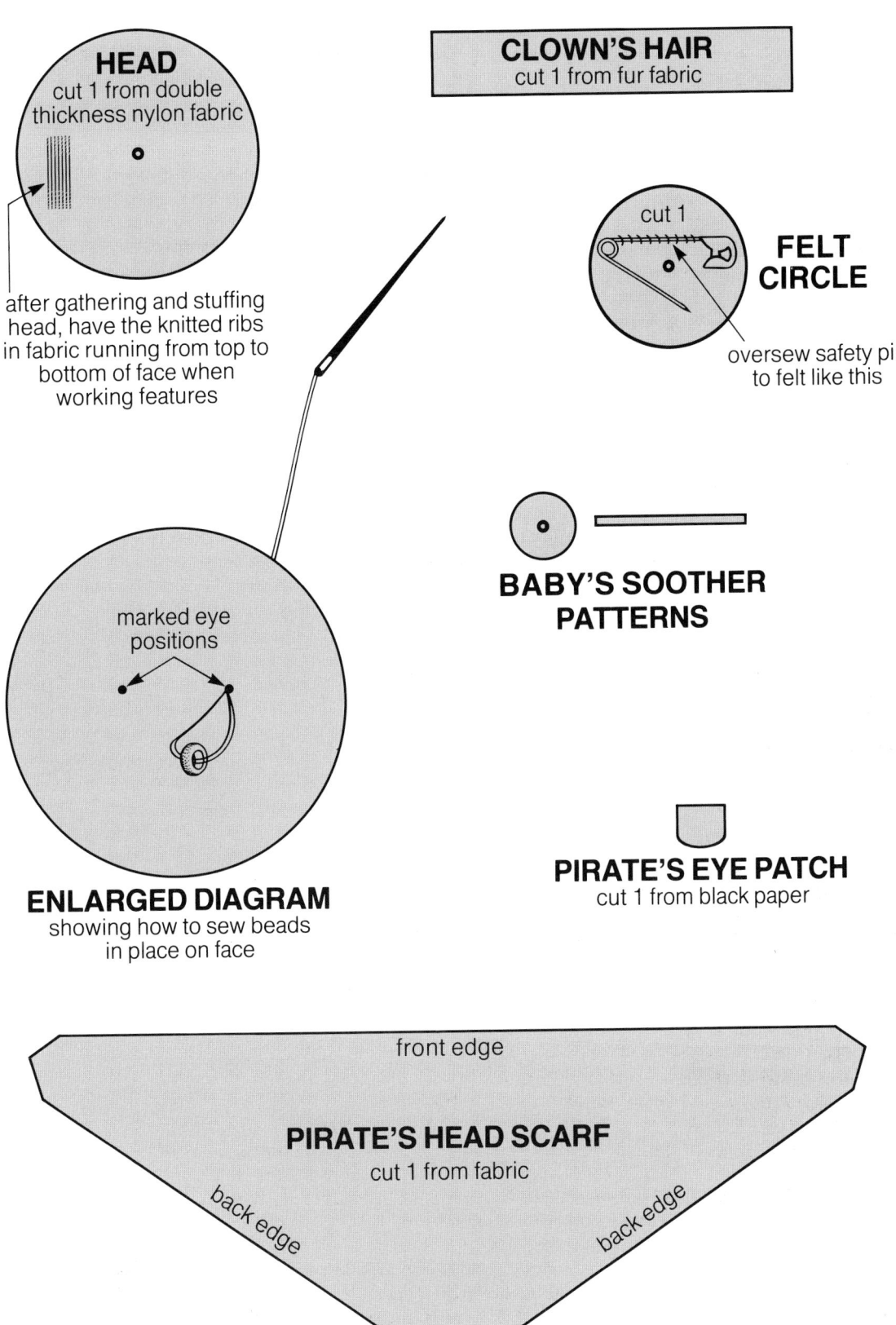

HEAD
cut 1 from double
thickness nylon fabric

after gathering and stuffing
head, have the knitted ribs
in fabric running from top to
bottom of face when
working features

CLOWN'S HAIR
cut 1 from fur fabric

cut 1

**FELT
CIRCLE**

oversew safety pin
to felt like this

**BABY'S SOOTHER
PATTERNS**

marked eye
positions

ENLARGED DIAGRAM
showing how to sew beads
in place on face

PIRATE'S EYE PATCH
cut 1 from black paper

front edge

PIRATE'S HEAD SCARF
cut 1 from fabric

back edge

back edge

COUNTRY COTTAGE TEA-COSY

Perhaps you can't afford that dream cottage in the country, but you can stitch up a miniature version which will keep your morning cuppa piping hot.

The cosy illustrated measures 26cm (10¼in) high, by 38cm (15in) across the base and it fits over a medium to large tea-pot.

I used fur fabric for the walls and roof to give extra insulation, but ordinary woven fabrics are just as suitable.

You will need: A 20×91cm (8×36in) strip of yellow fur fabric for the walls; 22×34cm (9×14in) piece of tan fur fabric for roof; 30×91cm (12×36in) piece of plain fabric for lining and the same amount of plastic foam sheeting, about 5mm (¼in) thick, for the padding; scraps of fabric, non-fray if possible (or use felt); scrap of green fur fabric; scrap of net fabric; short lengths of braid, lace edging and trimming; rosebud and guipure flower trimming; adhesive; yellow pen or pencil (optional).

Notes: The outline of the tea-cosy is too large to print on the page, but it can easily be drawn full-size from the diagram given. Patterns for all the appliqué pieces on the walls are given full-size for tracing off the page.

They are drawn to the exact size required, so if you are using fabrics which fray, then add 5mm (¼in) to all the edges which are not lapped by other pieces. Turn this allowance to wrong side and tack, before sewing pieces in place.

The door and window details on the diagram are only given to indicate the approximate position of the appliquéd pieces, but you don't need to be too fussy about this.

Specific types of fabric are only mentioned occasionally for the appliqué pieces – for other pieces use whatever you have on hand.

If you are using fur fabric, cut out the wall pieces with the smooth stroke of the fur pile going in the direction shown on the diagram. For the roof, this does not matter, because front and back are cut in one piece.

Safety note: Tea-cosies are now made in so many different forms and some even represent animals. Consequently, it is important to be aware that a child might think the tea-cosy is a toy house which could be dragged off the table for play. It is safest, therefore, to keep the cosy in a cupboard when there are young children around.

To draw the pattern

Copy the outline of the cosy from the diagram to the sizes given.

Cut this full-size pattern at the dotted line shown on the diagram to separate the roof section from the wall. Now glue a straight strip of paper to these cut edges, to add an extra 5mm (¼in) on each edge for the seam.

To make the pieces

For the roof, pin your pattern to the wrong side of the fur fabric and draw a line on the fabric level with the top edge of roof. Cut out the fabric level with pattern at side and lower edges *only*. Remove the pattern and pin it to fabric again, having the top edge exactly level with and on the other side of, the marked line. Cut out at side and lower edges as before, so that you now have front and back of roof in one piece.

Cut out two wall pieces, then join top edge of each one to lower edges of roof, taking 5mm (¼in) seams. Appliqué pieces to front wall of cottage first.

The front wall

Cut the door and letter-box, then stitch letter-box to door. Sew on a guipure flower for the door-knob. Sew door in place at the approximate position shown on diagram, having one short edge just above lower edge of wall. Stitch the edges of lengths of braid to each side of door, just lapping them over the door fabric. Cut the doorstep and sew it in place, having one long edge level with lower edge of wall.

Cut the porch and sew it above the door, having the upper edge level with roof. Cut the window piece by the outer edge, then cut the piece from the centre by the line shown on pattern to leave a frame. Cut a piece of net fabric a bit smaller than the outer edge of frame. Hold net to wrong side of frame with dabs of glue. Place strips of lace trimming behind net for the curtains and glue in place as for net. Cut a piece of black felt or fabric same size as the net and place it on wrong side of frame, holding with dabs of glue as before. Now stitch all around the inner edge of window frame to hold all the pieces together. Sew outer edge of window frame to wall at position shown in the diagram.

Cut two shutters, then stitch them to sides of window, just lapping them over the side edges of frame.

Cut window-box, then stitch it under window, having one long edge level with lower edge of window frame.

Cut a few irregular strips of green fur fabric and sew them to lower edge of wall here and there.

Sew on trimmings as follows. Braid or trimming to porch and window-box. Flowers above window-box. Rosebud trimming to side of door and over porch. Guipure flowers to grass. If you have a yellow pen or pencil handy, use it to colour centres of these flowers.

The back wall

Make all window pieces as for front and sew them in place nearer to centre than for front window. Add all other trimmings as for front wall.

To make up the cosy

Fold cosy in half at marked line at centre of roof with wrong side outside. Join sides, taking 5mm (¼in) seams. Turn cosy right side out.

Take your original roof and wall patterns and trim off the extra strips of paper which you added for the seam. Join the pattern pieces at these edges with bits of sticky tape. Cut two lining pieces using this pattern, but add 1cm (⅜in) to each one at the top edge of roof. Turn this 1cm (⅜in) extra to wrong side of each piece and tack. Join the side edges of the lining pieces, taking 5mm (¼in) seams. Leave wrong side out. Slip lining (wrong side out) over cosy (right side out). Join lining to cosy all round lower edges, taking a 1cm (⅜in) seam. Turn lining to inside of cosy, then turn the complete cosy wrong side out so that right side of lining is outside.

Cut two pieces of foam using the same pattern as for the lining and cut the foam level with all the edges of the pattern. After removing the pattern, trim 1cm (⅜in) off all the edges of each foam piece. Now slip each foam piece between the lining and fabric and catch them together along the top edges. Oversew the turned in top edges of lining together. Catch this edge of lining to the foam and the fur fabric roof with long stitches just to hold in place. Turn the completed cosy right side out.

CHRISTMAS CRIB

I really enjoyed designing this nativity scene, using only materials which might be on hand, or which could easily be purchased at the last minute before Christmas. The standing figures are about 11cm (4¼in) high and the stable floor measures 20 × 32cm (8 × 12½in).

The garments are mostly made from felt, plus a few odd bits of fabric and trimmings to add interest. I covered the stable pieces with hessian and coarsely woven brown curtain material to provide a plain home-spun background which sets off the simplicity of the figures.

For the figures you will need: Thin card which bends easily without cracking (you can use up old Christmas or birthday cards); oddments of felt and fabrics; flesh-coloured and brown felt; a little stuffing and cotton wool; three wooden cocktail-sticks; a piece of twig for Joseph's staff; narrow shoe-lace (the tubular kind); two pipe-cleaners; thin cord; fancy braids or gift-wrapping braid; thin polyester wadding or cotton wool for the lambs; for the kings' gifts you can use fancy beads, buttons, bits of junk jewellery, ear-rings or chunky necklace clasps; a black pencil (not ordinary lead pencil, but the type used for colouring); red and black thread; a white paper tissue for baby's shawl; adhesive.

For the stable you will need: Pieces of strong corrugated reinforced cardboard cut off grocery boxes; plain textured fabrics for covering the pieces; silver card, or kitchen foil and card for the star; adhesive.

Notes: Patterns for the figures and lambs are all given full-size for tracing off the page. For the stable, measurements are quoted in the instructions. Before cutting out the hand, beard and lamb's ear pieces, treat the felt with adhesive as described at the beginning of the book.

When gluing pieces together, for example the back edges of the body, hold in place with pins until the adhesive dries. All the pieces are glued together except for the kings' head-dresses and Mary's shawl where there are small seams to be stitched.

Joseph

Cut the body shape from card. Gently bend the card, easing it into a smooth cone shape with the back edges lapping over each other. Take care not to have any sharp angles or bends in the card. Open up the cone, then glue the right side (the *outside* surface of the cone) onto the wrong side of a piece of fabric. Cut out the fabric 5mm (¼in) larger all round than the card. Clip fabric at upper curved edges, then turn and stick the extra fabric to the other side of the card. Re-form the cone shape, lapping and gluing the back edges of body 1cm (⅜in).

Cut the robe from felt, using the body pattern. Wrap it around body from back to front, then glue upper edges to upper edges of body. Cut two sleeves from felt to match the robe. Fold each one at dotted line shown on pattern, then glue the upper and the back edges together. Glue upper edges of sleeves to sides of body at position shown on pattern.

Cut hands from two layers of flesh-coloured felt glued together. Put the hands inside wrist edges of sleeves, as shown in the colour photograph, then glue them in place. Bend the right sleeve at the 'elbow' and glue it to robe to hold in this position. Glue a 9cm (3½in) length of twig to right hand, curling hand around it.

Cut the head from flesh-coloured felt and mark on the black dot, as shown on the pattern. Gather around the edge of head, stuff firmly, then pull up gathers as tightly as possible and fasten off. Break one cocktail-stick in half and use one half only. Pierce head with pointed end of stick at the marked dot, as shown in the diagram. Remove stick and spread point with glue, then push into head again.

Spread glue inside upper edges of body, then push cocktail-stick inside it at the centre so that head touches body. Press back and front upper edges of body together, securing the cocktail-stick. At this stage the head may be tilted to one side, as in photograph.

Mark position of eyes first with pins, then ordinary pencil, half-way down face and 8mm (⁵⁄₁₆in) apart, then proceed as follows. Make sure black pencil point is sharp. Moisten point, then push it into felt at marked position and twist around to make a perfect circle. Cut the beard from folded brown felt, placing edge indicated on pattern to fold in felt. Glue beard to face, leaving only the lower edge free.

Cut the head-dress from white felt. Gather around at dotted line shown on pattern, pull up gathers to fit top of head, then fasten off. Stick to top of head, then spread a little glue on inside of remainder of head-dress. On the right side, pinch the felt into folds all round. Glue thin cord around gathering thread.

Shepherd

Make exactly as for Joseph, varying the colours of fabric and felt. For the crook, cut a 12cm (4¾in) length of pipe-cleaner and push it inside a length of shoe-lace. Trim shoe-lace to length, then seal the ends with adhesive. Bend one end to crook shape, then glue to hand as illustrated in the photograph.

Three kings

Make bodies, robes and sleeves as for Joseph, but stick trimmings down the front edges and wrist edges of robes as illustrated. Make hands and heads as for Joseph also, using brown felt for one king and making another with a white beard. Work a small black stitch for mouth on the white beard. Bend sleeves slightly at 'elbows' and stick to robes to hold in position as illustrated, then glue a gift to each of the kings' hands.

For each king, cut a pair of head-dress pieces from fabric. Join back edges at seam stitching line shown on pattern. Turn in all the remaining raw edges 3mm (⅛in) and glue down. Glue head-dress to head and to the robe at the shoulders.

For the red and the yellow king's crowns, glue a strip of braid around top of head. For the green king, cut the crown from fabric using the pattern. Turn in raw edge 3mm (⅛in) and gather. Pull up gathers to fit around top of head as illustrated, then fasten off. Stuff crown lightly, then sew in place on head. Glue trimming around lower edge of crown.

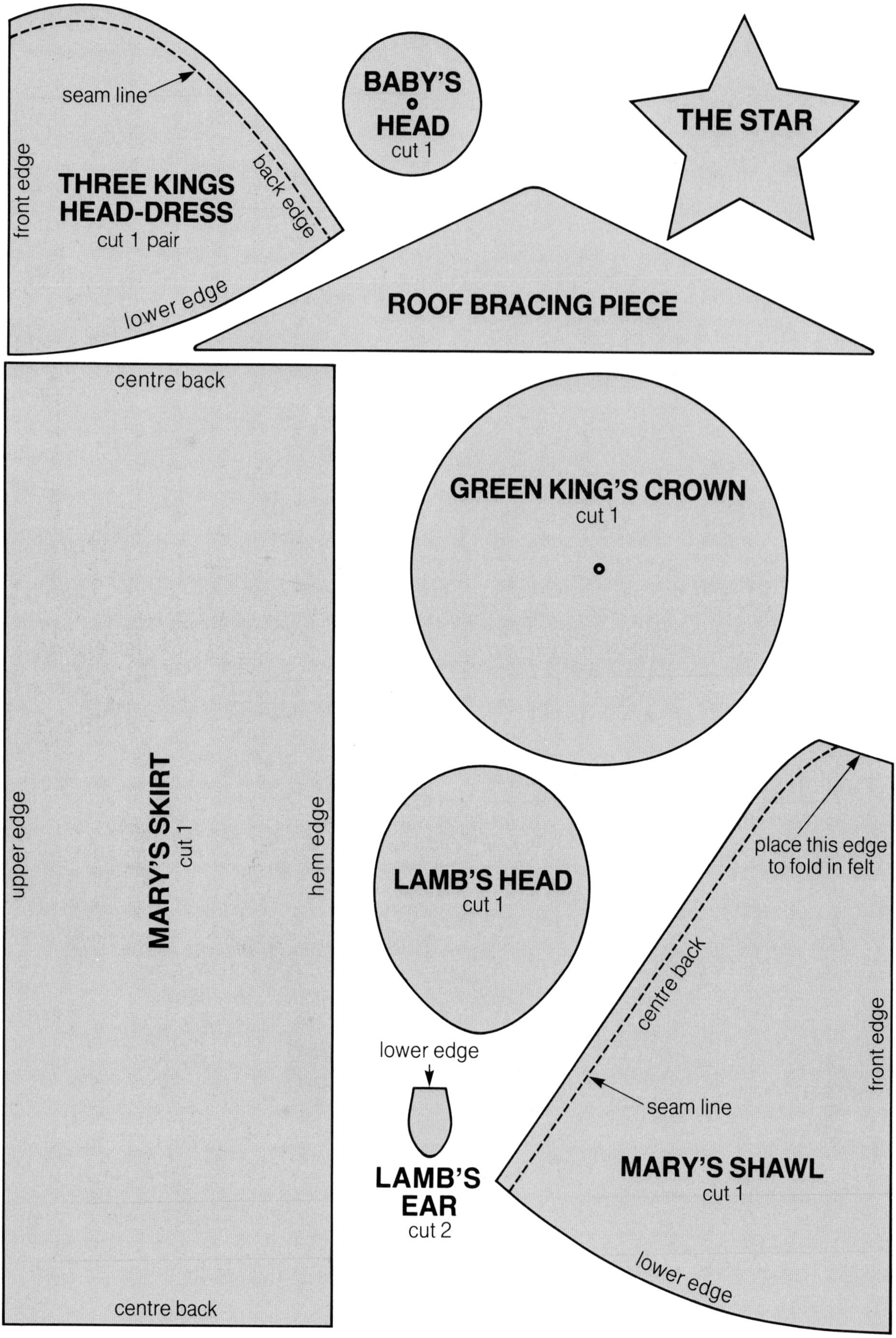

THREE KINGS
HEAD-DRESS
cut 1 pair

front edge

seam line

back edge

lower edge

BABY'S
HEAD
cut 1

THE STAR

ROOF BRACING PIECE

centre back

GREEN KING'S CROWN
cut 1

MARY'S SKIRT
cut 1

upper edge

hem edge

LAMB'S HEAD
cut 1

lower edge

LAMB'S
EAR
cut 2

place this edge
to fold in felt

centre back

seam line

front edge

MARY'S SHAWL
cut 1

lower edge

centre back

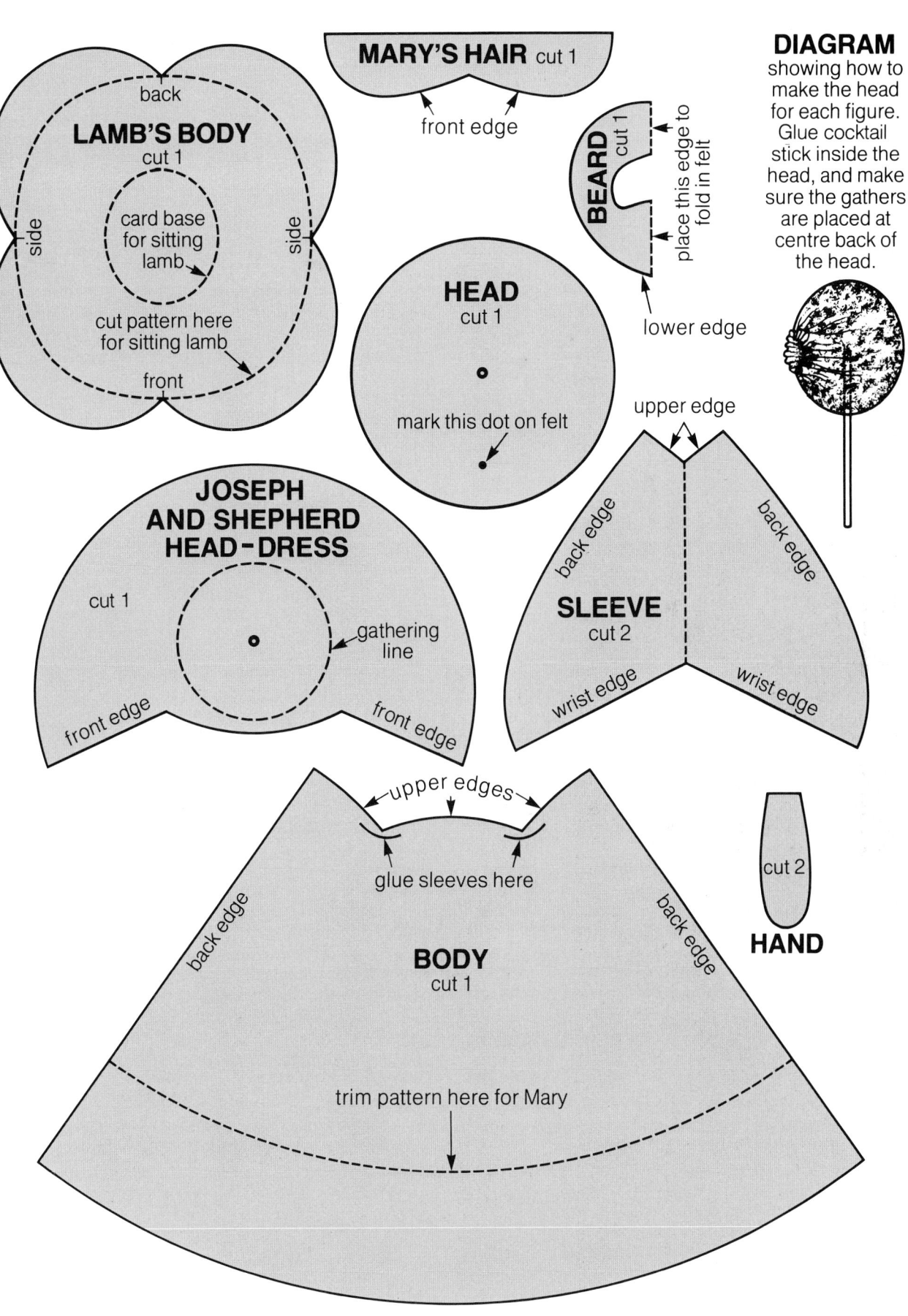

MARY'S HAIR cut 1

front edge

BEARD cut 1

place this edge to fold in felt

lower edge

DIAGRAM
showing how to make the head for each figure. Glue cocktail stick inside the head, and make sure the gathers are placed at centre back of the head.

LAMB'S BODY
cut 1

back

side

side

card base for sitting lamb

cut pattern here for sitting lamb

front

HEAD
cut 1

mark this dot on felt

JOSEPH AND SHEPHERD HEAD-DRESS

cut 1

gathering line

front edge

front edge

SLEEVE
cut 2

upper edge

back edge

back edge

wrist edge

wrist edge

upper edges

glue sleeves here

back edge

back edge

BODY
cut 1

trim pattern here for Mary

cut 2

HAND

Mary

Trim the body pattern along the dotted line indicated. Cut body from card, cover with felt and form to shape as for other figures. Make sleeves (from same colour felt), then head and hands and attach them all as for Joseph. Using black thread, work V-shapes for eyes and a short red stitch for mouth. Cut the hair strip from brown felt and glue it over head from side to side, having curved front edges at sides of face.

Cut the skirt piece from felt to match body. Lap and stick the centre back edges. Carefully stretch the hem edge to make it flare out. Glue the upper edge at centre back, to back of figure 1cm (⅜in) below upper edge of body. Now gather remainder of upper edge of skirt and pull up gathers to fit figure at front, 2.5cm (1in) below upper edge of body. Fasten off thread, then catch gathers to body. To form the 'knees', push a pad of cotton wool inside skirt at front.

Cut the shawl from folded felt, placing short top edge of pattern to the fold as indicated. Join centre back edges at seam stitching line, as shown on the pattern. Press seam open. Stretch lower edge in same way as for skirt. Glue the shawl to head and to body as shown in the photograph (p. 108).

Baby

Cut baby's head from flesh-coloured felt, then gather and stuff as for other figures, noting that gathers will be at back of head as before. Mark on tiny dots for eyes and work a small red stitch for mouth.

Cut a 10cm (4in) square off the paper tissue and fold a little of one corner over. Glue back of head to centre of this corner so that folded edge will wrap around head. Put a little roll of cotton wool below head for body.

Wrap the tissue around baby, gluing it in place here and there. Place baby on Mary's lap and glue her hands around him as shown in the photograph.

Lambs

The lambs are made from polyester wadding, but if this is not on hand you can substitute cotton wool if treated as follows. Pull a thin even layer off a roll of cotton wool, then spray the surface with hair-spray and leave to dry. Make the lambs from either.

For the standing lamb, cut out the body, using the outline of the pattern, then gather all around the edges of curves. Pull up gathers and stuff, taking care to fill each curved corner with stuffing to form the legs. Pull up gathers tightly and fasten off. Oversew, from centre front of body to centre back across the gathers, pulling thread tight, then repeat from side to side and fasten off. This will define the legs a little more.

Cut out lamb's head, gather around the edge, stuff, pull up tight and fasten off. Sew gathered back of head to front of body, referring to the photograph as a guide to positioning. Cut two ears from white felt. Fold them

in half at lower edges and glue. Stick the ears to sides of head. Mark eyes with pencil in the same way as for figures.

For the tail, cut a 3cm (1¼in) length of pipe-cleaner. Glue a small strip of wadding or cotton wool around it. Use scissors point to pierce a small hole at centre back of body, then glue 1cm (⅜in) of tail inside it. Curl tail as illustrated.

For the sitting lamb, trim the body pattern along the dotted line indicated. Gather around the edge and stuff, but before pulling gathers right up, cut the base piece from card (shown by dotted line on pattern) and insert it into body. Pull up gathers and fasten off. Make and attach head, ears and tail as for standing lamb.

Stable

For the floor, cut two 20×32cm (8×12½in) pieces of card and glue them together. Put dots of glue here and there on one side of card and place on a piece of fabric. Cut out fabric 3cm (1¼in) larger all around than card. Turn this extra fabric over to the other side of card and stick down, trimming fabric at corners so that it turns neatly.

For the side wall pieces, cut two 6×14cm (2⅜×5½in) strips of card and cover them with fabric in the same way as for floor. Glue one short edge of each wall to sides of floor at the back, having wrong sides of walls facing each other. Push pins through the walls and into floor to hold in place until glue dries.

Now cut another two wall pieces 1cm (⅜in) shorter than the first two. Cover with fabric as before, then stick them to the first wall pieces, having wrong sides of walls together.

For the roof, cut a 9×40cm (3½×15¾in) strip of card. Bend the strip at the exact centre to form the apex shape of roof. Cover right side of roof with fabric as for walls, keeping the card in the bent position when doing this. Neaten underside of roof by gluing on a strip of felt or paper to cover the raw edges of the fabric.

Now cut two roof bracing pieces from card and glue them together. Cover one side of card with fabric as for the other pieces. Cut another piece from thin card and glue it to the wrong side to cover the raw edges of fabric. Stick sloping edges of roof bracing piece inside apex of roof, about 2.5cm (1in) away from one long edge of roof (this edge will face to the front).

Now place roof in position on top of walls. Have the short ends extending equally beyond walls, and long back edge of roof level with back edges of walls. Mark wall positions on underside of roof. Remove roof and spread glue on marked positions and on top edges of walls. Replace roof and hold with pins until glue dries.

Cut the star from silver card, gluing a few layers together if necessary. Alternatively, cover plain card with kitchen foil. Glue star in place.

Colour photograph on page 108

BEADED SACHETS

These miniscule draw-string bags, just 7cm (2¾in) high, are made extra special by adding a couple of pretty beads and some shiny narrow ribbon. You can fill them with lavender or pot-pourri to slip into a lingerie drawer, or hang the ribbon loops over coathangers.

You will need: Lavender flowers or pot-pourri; scraps of thin soft fabric; for each bag a 50cm (20in) length of 3mm (⅛in) wide ribbon (or you can substitute cord); two small beads with holes large enough to pass the ribbon through.

Note: Seams are as stated in the instructions.

To make

For a pattern, cut a rectangle of paper measuring 9×11cm (3½×4¼in). If making a lot of bags, then pin the pattern to several layers and cut them all out at once, for speed.

Cut a 14cm (5½in) length of ribbon and fold it in half, then make a knot at about the centre of the double ribbon length. Thread a bead onto the folded end of ribbon and push it against the knot.

Join the short edges of one fabric strip, taking a 5mm (¼in) seam. Leave wrong side out. Gather round, 5mm (¼in) away from one raw edge and pull up gathers slightly. Put the ribbon *inside* the bag, with folded end protruding through gathers as shown in the diagram. Pull up gathers tightly around ribbon, just above the bead, and fasten off. Sew through gathers and ribbon to hold in place.

Now turn up the remaining raw edge 1.5cm (⅝in) and gather round 1cm (⅜in) away from the fold, as shown in the diagram, but do not pull up gathers. Turn this edge up, pulling the ribbon ends and bead through, to turn the bag right side out. Fill as far as gathers with lavender or pot-pourri.

For the ribbon loop at top of bag, cut an 18cm (7in) length of ribbon, then fold and knot at centre as for the other ribbon. Thread the bead onto *ends* of ribbon and push it against the knot. Slip the ribbon ends inside the gathered top edge of bag, pull up gathers tightly around the ribbon ends so that the bead is visible above the gathers, then fasten off. Sew ribbon in place through gathers.

Tie the remaining length of ribbon in a bow around these gathers, then sew centre of bow to fabric so that it cannot be undone.

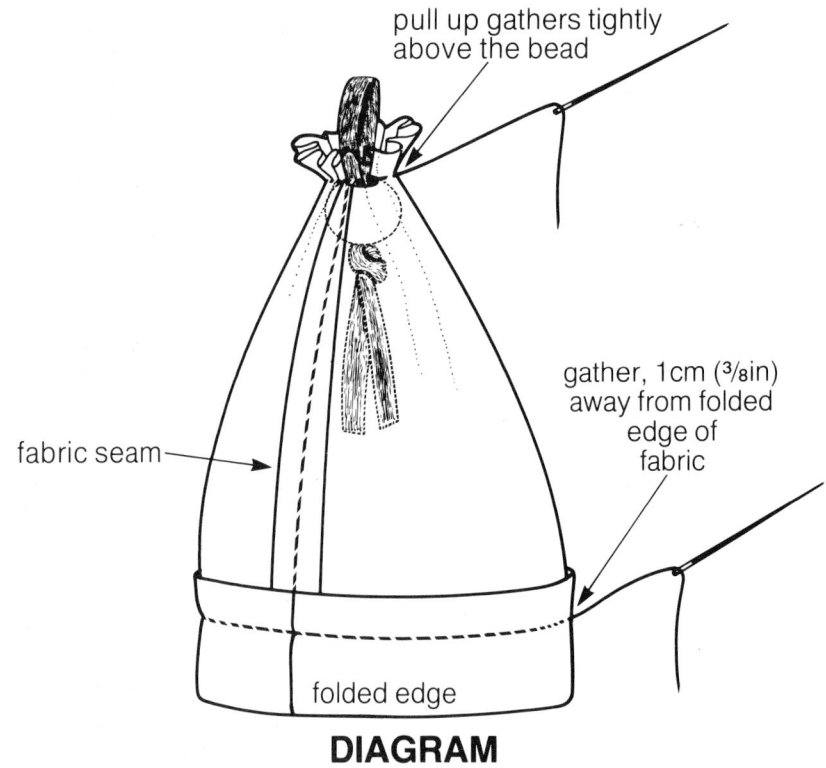

pull up gathers tightly above the bead

gather, 1cm (⅜in) away from folded edge of fabric

fabric seam

folded edge

DIAGRAM

GIFT BASKETS

Pretty packaging is all-important for a special gift or when you are selling home-made sweetmeats. These little baskets are extremely quick and easy to make (without any sewing), from Binca embroidery fabric (USA: 6 count Aida).

The finished baskets measure 7–10cm (3–4in) across and you can fill them with small soaps, bath-salts, home-made sweets and biscuits, pot-pourri and fresh or dried flowers. You can also make – from a yellow duster – some realistic tangerine sachets filled with lavender.

For the baskets you will need: Corrugated reinforced type of card cut off a grocery box; oddments of Binca, ribbon and braid; adhesive.

For the tangerine sachets you will need: A yellow duster as near to a tangerine shade as possible – one duster will make about twelve sachets; lavender flowers; stuffing; scraps of orange and green felt; length of white knitting yarn.

Notes: There is no seaming on the baskets, all pieces being glued together. When cutting out Binca pieces, you can follow the woven strands to get perfectly straight edges.

THE OBLONG BASKET

For the base pattern, cut a 6 × 10cm (2¼ × 4in) strip of paper. Fold it into quarters, then round off the outer corners. Open up pattern, then draw round it onto a piece of card. Cut out, then cut two more card pieces in same way. Glue all the card pieces together to form a firm base.

For the basket sides piece, cut a 5 × 32cm (2 × 12½in) strip of Binca. Fold it in half along the length, bringing the long edges together. Press the strip as folded, then glue the long edges together.

Now stick these glued edges around the edges of cardboard base, having short ends of Binca overlapping at the centre of the one long edge of base. Trim any excess on the overlap, leaving about 5mm (¼in), then glue this overlap in place.

For the basket handle, cut a 4 × 17cm (1½ × 6¾in) strip of Binca. Fold in the long edges to meet each other at the centre of the strip, then press. Glue the long edges in place against the side of the basket.

Stick the ends of the handle to outside of basket at the centre of the long edges, having the short edges of the handle level with the cardboard base. Glue a ribbon bow to each side of the handle, as shown in the colour photograph overleaf.

The tangerine sachets

The basket is just large enough to hold two sachets. For each tangerine, cut a 12cm (4¾in) diameter circle from the duster. Gather round, 5mm (¼in) away from the raw edge. Pull up gathers slightly and half-fill circle with lavender flowers. Continue filling with stuffing to make a nice rounded shape. Pull up gathers tightly and fasten off.

To make the stalk, thread a long needle with a length of white yarn and knot the ends of yarn together. Trim off yarn ends close to knot. Put a dab of adhesive on the knot and twirl it with your fingers to smooth it.

Cut a tiny irregular-shaped bit of green felt and place it on the centre top of tangerine. Take the needle through the felt and tangerine and bring it out at the gathers. Pull yarn tightly, to depress stalk into tangerine slightly, then fasten off yarn at gathers.

Cut a 2.5cm (1in) diameter circle of orange felt and glue or sew it underneath tangerine to cover the raw edges. Smooth out any creases in sachet by rubbing it against a warm iron.

You can crumple a paper tissue inside the basket if desired, before putting in the sachets.

THE SQUARE BASKET

Make exactly as given for the oblong basket, but use the following measurements.

For the base pattern, cut an 8cm (3¼in) square of paper, rounding off corners as before. For the basket sides, cut an 8 × 32cm (3¼ × 13in) strip of Binca. For the handle, cut a 5 × 22cm (2 × 8¾in) strip of Binca.

After gluing on the handle as for the oblong basket, stick strips of braid around upper and lower edges of basket sides, as illustrated in the photograph (p. 116).

THE ROUND BASKET

Make in the same way as for the oblong basket, but use the following measurements.

For the base pattern, cut a 9cm (3½in) diameter

circle of paper. For side of basket, cut a 9×30cm (3½×12in) strip of Binca. For the handle, cut a 5×26cm (2×10¼in) strip of Binca.

After gluing on the handle, stick a strip of braid along the full length of the handle and also around the lower edge of basket, as illustrated in the photograph above.

KITCHEN PAD AND PINNY

Stitch a practical apron, with a strong pocket for holding clothes-pegs, then glue together a smart note-board to hang on the kitchen wall from the bits left over.

The note-pad and a pencil both slip into handy ribbon loops so that they can be removed or renewed. The instructions are written to suit any size of pad.

You will need: 50cm (⅝yd) of 91cm (36in) wide printed cotton fabric; 60cm (¾yd) of 91cm (36in) wide toning fabric, either spotted or plain; 30cm (⅜yd) of fancy lace edging; scrap of ribbon; a note-pad – the one used measured 10×15cm (4×6in); a pencil; pieces of thin strong card; craft knife, or sharp pen-knife; adhesive.

Note: 1cm (⅜in) seams are allowed on the apron pieces throughout.

APRON

Cut a 50×46cm (19½×18in) piece of printed fabric, noting that the larger measurement will form the apron *width*.

For the pocket, cut two 22×30cm (8¾×12in) pieces of the toning fabric. Sew the lace edging to the right side of one of these pieces, 3cm (1¼in) away from one long edge. Join the pocket pieces all around the edges, leaving a gap for turning. Trim corners, turn right side out and press, then slip stitch gap.

Pin the pocket to apron, placing it centrally across width, and having upper edge 8cm (3in) down from top edge of apron. Stitch side and lower edge of pocket in place. Stitch again, 1cm (⅜in) within the first line of stitching.

For the borders at the side edges of apron, cut two 8×46cm (3×18in) strips of the toning fabric. Take one of the strips and pin one long edge to side edge of apron, having *right* side of strip against *wrong* side of apron and the raw edges level. Stitch as pinned. Press seam and strip away from apron. Turn in the remaining long edge of strip 1cm (⅜in) and press. Turn this edge over to right side of apron and pin it to printed fabric just beyond seam stitching line as shown in Diagram 1 overleaf. Stitch as pinned. Sew on the other side strip in same way.

Bind the lower edge of apron in the same way, using an 8cm (3in) wide strip of fabric. Make the strip the same length as the lower edge of apron (including borders) and add 1cm (⅜in) extra at each end of strip for turning in and neatening these raw edges.

For the apron waist-band, cut two 8×91cm (3×36in) strips of toning fabric and join them at one short edge, to make one long strip. Press seam open. Note that this seam will be at the centre front of apron.

Gather the top edge of apron along the printed fabric only, leaving the borders straight. Pull up gathers to measure 28cm (11in). Now pin centre seam of waist-band to centre of gathered edge of apron, having *right* side of band against *wrong* side of apron and the raw edges level. Continue pinning band to gathers on either side of centre. Stitch as pinned. Press seam and strip away from apron.

Turn in all the remaining raw edges of waist-band 1cm (⅜in) and press. Fold waist-band in half along the length, having right side outside, then stitch across the ends and through long edges, enclosing gathered edge of apron at centre, as shown in Diagram 2.

NOTE-BOARD

Cut a piece of card to suit your note-pad size, making it about 3cm (1¼in) larger all round than the pad. Round off the corners slightly, drawing around the curved edge of a small lid or bottle to do this equally at each corner. Cut an identical piece of card (you can draw round the first one), and lay it aside until later.

Place card on wrong side of a piece of the toning fabric and draw around it. Cut out fabric about 1cm (⅜in) larger all round than marked line. Place card on wrong side of fabric again, then turn the surplus fabric

on to other side of card and glue down, clipping fabric at corners so that it turns neatly.

Place the note-pad centrally on right side of board and mark a short line on fabric at either side of board, at top edge. Use craft knife or pen-knife to cut a slit through fabric and board at marked lines, to suit the width of your ribbon. Push the ends of a length of ribbon through slit to back of card, keeping it taut.

place it on a piece of fabric (for wallpaper), cut about 2cm (¾in) larger all round than the card. Turn this extra fabric to the other side of the card and glue in place, keeping fabric taut as you do this. Glue another piece of card to wrong side of wall to cover the raw edges of fabric. Do not assemble the pieces at this stage.

Fireplace

Take two of the match-boxes and cover them with brick-effect paper by gluing strips of paper around the slide-on cover of each one.

For the grate, take the tray from another match-box (you won't need the slide-on cover), then cut it in half along the length. Use one half only and note that the original *bottom* of the tray will be the *bottom* of the grate. Colour the grate inside and out with black felt-tipped pen. Glue black braid around the long and short sides of the grate. Fix the paper fastener through at the centre of the long side (centre front) of grate, or sew on a bead. Now glue printed paper-cutting of coal fire in the grate, crumpling the paper slightly.

To assemble the fireplace pieces, place the grate between the brick-covered match-boxes, as indicated on the floor pattern, then glue them together. Glue this completed piece to the floor at the position shown on the pattern.

Place the wall in position at right angles to the back of the floor and mark the fireplace opening on the wall fabric. Colour this area of wall with a black felt-tipped pen, then glue on a paper-cutting of coal-fire flames.

Now glue the wall in place against the floor, spreading glue on the back of the brick-covered fireplace pieces as well as along the lower edge of wall. Keep pressing in place until glue has a good hold.

Mantelpiece

Glue the remaining match-boxes together, end to end, pushing the inner trays in towards each other when you do this to get a good grip.

Place the mantelpiece on a piece of thin card, having the largest surface of boxes against the card, then draw round it. Cut out the card strip. Glue on a piece of brown paper and colour it to resemble wood, as for the floor, then glue the card strip to the match-boxes. Glue the mantelshelf in place on the tops of the brick-covered pieces and to the wall.

Glue braid around the edges of mantelpiece at right angles, as shown in the photograph. I used two strips of different braids to get an extra pretty effect.

Tiled hearth

Cut a strip of white card (or glue white paper to card) for the hearth, the size shown on the pattern. Use an ordinary pencil, then a blue one, to mark into separate tiles, as shown. Use blue pencil to colour a design on each tile, as shown on the pattern. Place hearth in position. If there is a bit of floor-board showing between the fireplace pieces and the hearth, colour this with a black pen. Glue hearth in place, then use an orange pencil to shade a glow on the tiles, just in front of fire.

Fender

Cut a 1cm (⅜in) wide strip of card long enough to go around the front and side edges of tiled hearth. Colour card on both sides with a black pen. Bend it at corner positions to fit around hearth. Glue on a strip of gold braid, then stick fender in place.

Finishing touches

Glue the narrow braid all around the edges of the floor and wall, turning one long edge onto right side of card and the other long edge onto wrong side.

For the skirting-boards, cut two 2cm (¾in) wide pieces of card to fit wall at each side of fireplace, within the edges of braid. Colour skirting-boards as for floor. On one skirting piece cut a tiny rough semi-circle, for the mouse-hole. Before gluing skirtings in place, colour the wall behind the position of mouse-hole with a black pen.

Clock

Cut out a suitable size of clock face and glue it to a button or buckle. For a stand, glue one end of a strip of card to the back near the top. Bend the other end of card away from clock.

Pictures and books

Cut these from printed matter and glue onto card, then cut out card level with edges. Glue books on mantelpiece. To make the pictures look as though they are hanging on wall, glue a small piece of card to the back of each one, near to top, then glue them in place.

Cat's bowl of milk

Glue a circle of white paper into Smarties lid.

Vase of flowers

Spread glue on the ends of dried flower stalks and place them in a perfume bottle. Glue base of bottle in place. Glue glass button to mantelpiece also.

Plant

Push a lump of Plasticine into the toothpaste tube lid, then push dried grasses into Plasticine. Glue lid to the button, then stick button to floor.

Knitting

For the needles, cut the cocktail-sticks to 4cm (1½in) in length. Glue these cut ends into beads.

For the knitted piece, split a length of thin yarn (4-ply – USA: sportweight – is best) and use a split strand. With the finest gauge knitting-needles available, cast on a few stitches and knit a few rows. Transfer stitches onto one cocktail-stick needle, then wind the remaining end of yarn into a tiny ball. Secure the wound strands on ball by sewing backwards and forwards through it with matching sewing thread. Glue knitting to mantelpiece.

Rug

Cut three 3m (3¼yd) lengths of double knitting (USA: worsted weight) yarn. Fold them in half and sew together at folds with sewing thread, then leave this needle threaded. Plait the six strands together.

Now coil the plait round and round, starting at the folded end and using sewing thread to catch edges of plait together as you go. When you come to the end, tuck ends of yarn under rug and sew in place. Press rug lightly.

Letter

I actually managed to find an illustration of a letter in a magazine, but you can make one from brown paper.

THE CAT

Body

Pin body pattern to two layers of fleecy fabric, having right sides together. Stitch all round close to edge of pattern. Before removing pattern, mark the dots at the ends of slit line shown by pushing a pencil point through pattern and into fabric.

Remove pattern and cut out body 3mm (⅛in) away from stitching line. Cut slit from dot to dot in the marked fabric layer only. Turn body right side out through slit. Fill body with lentils, but not too firmly. Ladder stitch along lines shown on pattern, closing the slit. This will be underneath the body.

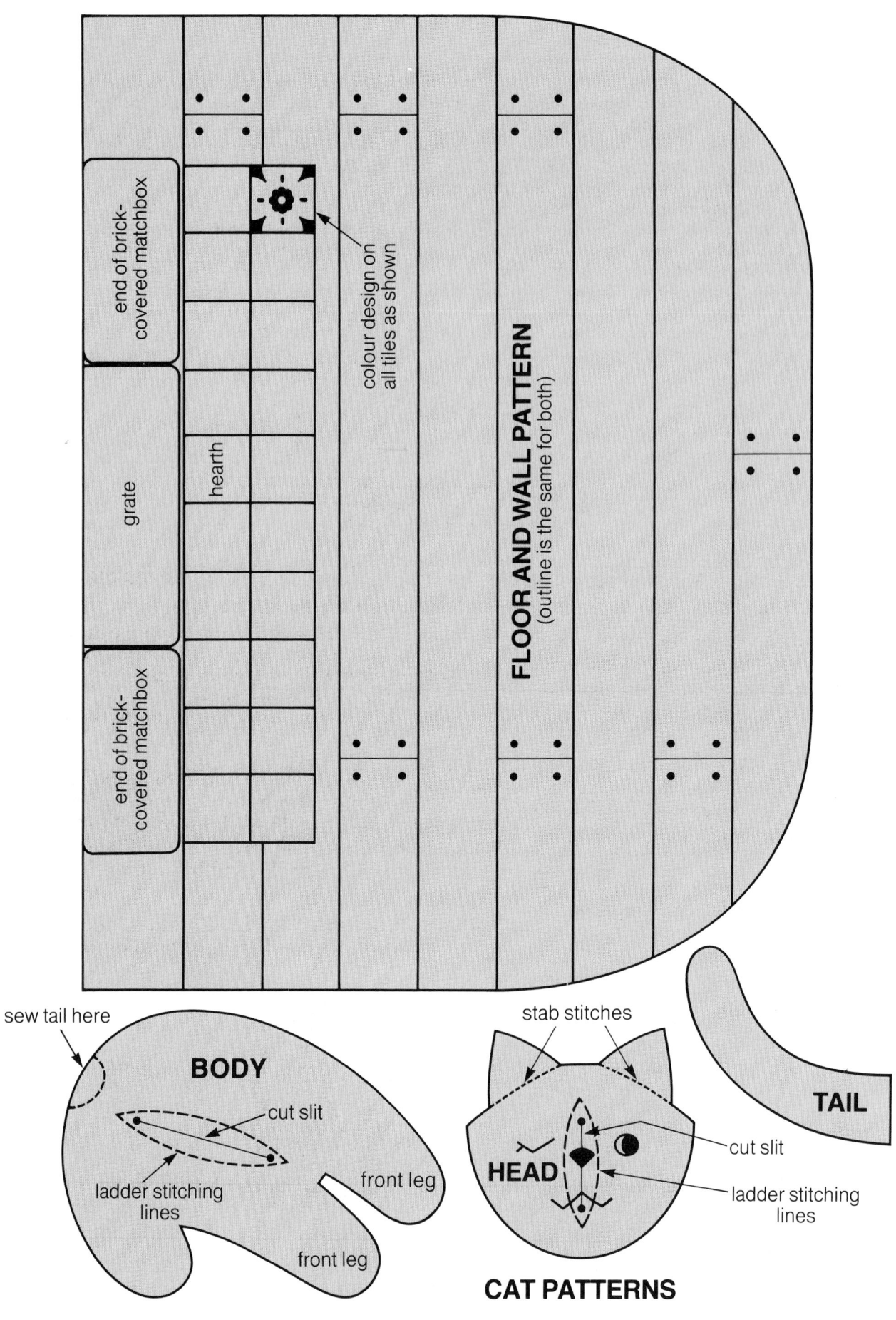

end of brick-covered matchbox

grate

hearth

end of brick-covered matchbox

colour design on all tiles as shown

FLOOR AND WALL PATTERN
(outline is the same for both)

sew tail here

BODY

cut slit

ladder stitching lines

front leg

front leg

stab stitches

HEAD

cut slit

ladder stitching lines

TAIL

CAT PATTERNS

Head

Stitch, cut slit and turn as for body. Before filling with lentils, work a row of tiny stab stitches at base of each ear, as shown on the pattern. Fill with lentils, then ladder stitch as for body, at the back of the head.

For the nose, cut a 3mm (⅛in) in diameter circle of pink felt (use leather punch if available) and cut to shape shown on the pattern. Glue to face.

To work the mouth and closed eye, use sewing thread and start and fasten off threads at back of head out of sight. Work mouth in pink and eye in black stitches, as shown on the pattern. Cut the other eye as for nose, from blue felt. Use a black pen to mark on a black circle for pupil, as shown, then glue eye in place.

Place back of head against front of body, having chin resting on front legs, as shown in the photograph. Ladder stitch head to body where it touches. Colour cheeks and lower portion of ears by rubbing with a red pencil. Tie ribbon bow around neck.

Tail

Pin tail pattern to fabric in same way as for body. Cut fabric level with straight edge of tail. Stitch all around edge of pattern, leaving short edges open. Remove pattern and cut out tail as for body.

To turn tail right side out, use tweezers to push in the end, then a knitting-needle to turn right through. Sew the open end of tail to position shown at back of cat.

PRETTY LITTLE BOXES

Don't throw away those lids off your empty aerosol-spray cans – you will need them to make these expensive-looking boxes! Covered with scraps of Liberty lawn fabric and trimmed with toning ribbon and lace, they make ideal containers for finger rings, ear-rings or a piece of precious jewellery. The boxes illustrated in the colour photograph (overleaf) measure 5cm (2in) across × 4cm (1½in) high, but the instructions are written to accommodate any variations in aerosol lid sizes.

You will need: Plastic lids from aerosol-spray cans (the kind with straight sides without a lower protruding rim); scraps of printed and plain fabric; thin polyester wadding, narrow ribbon and lace edging; very thin card (about greetings card thickness); thicker card (cuttings off washing-powder or breakfast cereal boxes); adhesive.

Notes: In order to avoid confusion in the instructions, the aerosol lid will be called *the box* throughout. Some aerosol lids have small vertical protruding ribs inside the rim, as shown in Diagram 1. If you are using a lid of this type, trim off the ribs with a craft knife.

To make the box

Cut a strip of fabric 2cm (¾in) wider than the depth of the box and long enough to go around it, plus a bit

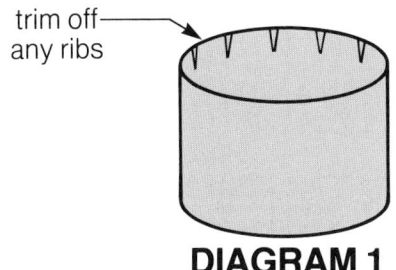

trim off any ribs

DIAGRAM 1

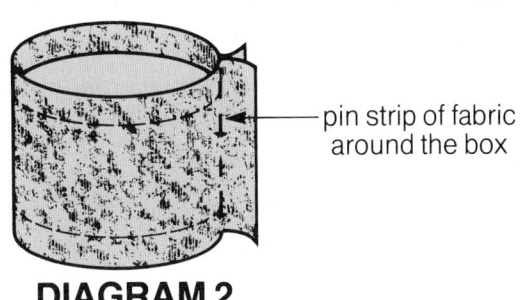

pin strip of fabric around the box

DIAGRAM 2

extra for seaming. Place it around the box, having wrong side of fabric outside, then pin short ends to fit, as shown in Diagram 2. Pull fabric off the box and stitch seam as pinned. Trim seam, then turn right side out.

Place the tube of fabric over the box again, with the raw edges protruding equally beyond the top and base of box. Turn and glue the upper raw edge of fabric to inside of box, then turn and glue the other raw edge underneath base.

Cut a strip of thin card to fit around the *inside* of the box, making it 5mm (¼in) narrower than the box depth. Place card strip on the wrong side of a piece of fabric cut 5mm (¼in) larger all round than the card. Turn the extra fabric to the other side of card and stick down, keeping the fabric taut. Glue lace trimming to the right side of one long edge of the strip. Spread a little adhesive inside the box, then put the strip in position.

To line the box base, cut a circle of thick card to fit inside the base of box (this will be slightly smaller than the outside diameter). Make a note of this circle size for use later on. Cut a circle of wadding the same size as the card, then a piece of plain fabric 5mm (¼in) larger all round than the card. Run a gathering thread around the edge of the fabric circle, but do not pull up. Place wadding at centre of circle, with card circle on top of wadding. Pull up gathers tightly, enclosing these circles, then fasten off. Glue this piece, gathered side down, inside the box base. Glue strips of ribbon and lace trimming around the outside of box at upper edge as shown in the photograph.

To make the box lid

Cut a circle of thick card the same diameter as the box. Cover this with a printed fabric circle (cut 1cm (⅜in) larger all round), in the same way as for the circle inside the box base, but using two layers of wadding.

Now cut three circles of thick card the same size as that noted when lining the box base. Glue card circles together and cover with fabric as before, using one layer of wadding only this time. Check that the finished circle will fit inside the box rim. Glue the finished circle to the box lid, with wrong sides facing.

Decorate the inside and outside of box lid with lace edging and ribbon bows, using the photograph as a guide to positioning the trimmings.

To cover the raw edges of fabric underneath the box, cut a circle of thin card to fit, cover with fabric as before, omitting the wadding. Glue the circle in place.

FAST FOOD

Serve up some fast food with a difference! Completely non-fattening, the egg-on-toast, burger and hot dog are, in fact, squashy bean-bags for playing catch. Even older members of the family may develop a craving for one of these no-calorie snacks – to use as a joke paperweight or conversation piece.

The food is life-size and for extra play value the various pieces can be taken apart.

You will need: Oddments of fabric in colours appropriate to the food; lentils for filling; small amount of stuffing and a 6cm (2½in) length of Velcro fastener for the egg-on-toast; fine-tipped permanent black marker pen; a green pencil (the type used for colouring).

Notes: All the different types of fabrics I used are mentioned in the instructions, but you can, of course, substitute others. The main bean-bag fabrics should be thick and strong enough to withstand throwing about. Thinner fabrics can also be used, provided the pieces are cut from double fabric. For example, the egg-white (made from white stockinette), is lined with white cotton fabric on the inside.

Most of the shapes are seamed all around the edges, then turned right side out through a slit cut in one of the pieces. If you are using double-thickness fabric for strength, tack the two layers together around the slit so that the beans will not slip between the layers when filling.

Make up a small paper funnel for pouring the beans into the bags and work over a basin – otherwise they will get everywhere!

Commercially made bean-bag toys contain plastic granules so that the toys can be washed. If you wish to use these, see the list of stockists at the end of the book.

Seams measuring 5mm (¼in) are allowed, unless otherwise stated. The hot-dog bun pattern is printed full-size. Measurements are given for all the other pieces.

POACHED EGG-ON-TOAST

For the toast, cut two 12cm (4¾in) squares of brown

velvety fabric, then cut a 4cm (1½in) long slit across the centre of one square. Join the squares all around the edges, rounding off the seam slightly at each corner. Trim the seam at the rounded corners, then turn right side out throught the slit.

Fill with ten dessert-spoons of lentils. Oversew the raw edges of the slit securely together. Sew on a 6cm (2½in) length of the hooked strip of Velcro to cover the slit.

For the egg-white, cut two 11cm (4¼in) diameter circles of white stockinette fabric (old T-shirt fabric will do). Cut a slit across the centre of one as for the toast. Join the circles all round, making a wavy seam line to get a slightly irregular shape. Turn right side out through the slit. Fill with six dessert-spoons of lentils. Finish off the slit and sew on the furry strip of Velcro as for the toast.

For the egg-yolk, cut an 8cm (3¼in) diameter circle of yellow stockinette fabric and run a gathering thread around the edge. Stuff the circle firmly, pulling up the gathers. Pull up gathers tightly, then fasten off. Place the yolk on top of the egg-white at the centre, having the gathered side facing down. Sew it securely in place. The egg can now be fixed to the toast with the Velcro strips.

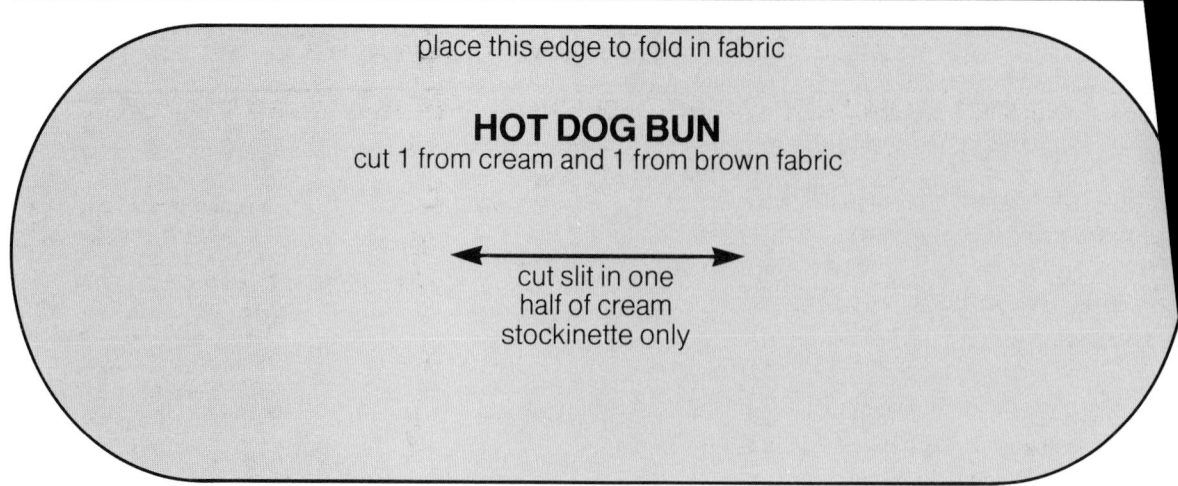

place this edge to fold in fabric

HOT DOG BUN
cut 1 from cream and 1 from brown fabric

cut slit in one
half of cream
stockinette only

BEEFBURGER

For each half of the bun, cut an 11cm (4¼in) diameter circle of mottled brown fabric and one of cream stockinette. Cut a 4cm (1½in) long slit across the centre of each cream circle. Join the circles in pairs all around the edges. Turn right side out through the slits and fill each one with seven dessert-spoons of lentils. Oversew the raw edges of each slit securely together.

To cover the slit at the centre of one of the bun pieces, cut an irregular-shaped piece of yellow velvet (to resemble mustard), making it large enough to cover the slit completely, plus a bit extra all round. Turn in and tack the raw edge, then sew to bun, having the right side up.

To cover the slit in the other bun piece, make a slice of onion. Cut two 7cm (2¾in) diameter circles of thin white fabric. Cut a tiny slit across the centre of one circle, then join them all around the edges. Trim the seam, turn right side out through the slit, then oversew the edges of the slit together. Use the black pen to lightly mark the rings on the right side of the onion slice, as shown in the colour photograph. Moisten the point of the green pencil, then use it to colour lightly around each ring. Sew the onion slice to the bun, slit side down.

For the beefburger, cut two 10cm (4in) diameter circles of textured brown fabric (I used a bit of bouclé-type coating material).

Make as for the bun halves, filling with four dessert-spoons of lentils.

For the splodge of tomato ketchup, cut a piece of red velvet and make as for the mustard. Sew it to the burger to cover the slit.

Make another slice of onion using two 6cm (2¼in) diameter circles of fabric, then sew this on top of the ketchup.

You can vary this design in several ways. To make a cheeseburger, cut two 9cm (3½in) squares of yellow fabric and make as for the other pieces, filling very lightly with lentils. Cover the slit with an onion ring, ketchup or mustard. Similarly, make the bun halves and add a square of cheese for a sandwich. You could also make bits of lettuce from crinkly fabric such as seersucker.

HOT DOG

For the bun, cut one piece from brown mottled fabric and one from cream stockinette, placing the edge indicated on the pattern to the fold in the fabric each time. Open up the pieces. Cut a slit in one half of the stockinette piece as shown on the pattern. Join the brown and cream pieces all around the edges. Clip the seam at the inner corners between the two bun halves.

Turn right side out through the slit, then fill the unslit half of the bun with four dessert-spoons of lentils. Now, keeping the lentils in this half, stitch through both layers of fabric along the length, between the two halves of the bun. Fill the remaining half of the bun with lentils as for the other half. Finish off the slit and add a splodge of ketchup to cover it in the same way as described for the burger.

For the sausage, cut an 8×20cm (3×8in) strip of tan needlecord fabric. Join the long edges of the strip, leaving a small gap at the centre of the seam for turning. Do not turn right side out just yet. To close the short ends, run a gathering thread around each one. Pull up the gathering threads tightly and fasten off. Oversew through the gathers to make quite secure.

Now turn the sausage right side out through the gap, then fill with lentils. Ladder stitch the gap in the seam. Make a splodge of mustard as for the burger, then sew it around the sausage.

For another idea, try making a chocolate éclair. Use lighter brown fabric for the outer layer of the bun, then add a slightly smaller piece of shiny dark-brown fabric to one side for the chocolate icing. Make the cream filling in the same way as for the sausage, shortening it to 14cm (5½in) and rounding off the ends when stitching, instead of gathering them up.

ENGLISH–AMERICAN GLOSSARY

...en off	Secure end of thread	Ric-rac	Rickrack
...fabric	Fake Fur	Snap fasteners	Snaps
...e wire	Very thin wire	Sticky tape	Transparent adhesive tape for sticking on paper
...pure flowers	Daisy lace, flower trim, flower decals	Stockinette	Cotton knit fabric
...n-on interfacing	Non-woven fusible interfacing	Strong buttonhole thread	Buttonhole twist
...ather punch	Hole punch	Tack	Baste
...ylon tights	Nylon pantyhose	UHU glue	Tacky glue or Slomons
...lasticine	Reusable modelling clay	Wooden dolly peg	Wooden clothes pin with knobbed tip
...olyester stuffing	Polyester fibrefill		
...olyester wadding	Polyester quilt batting	Zip fastener	Zipper

STOCKISTS

*A*ll the UK stockists listed will supply by mail order to the USA, Australia, etc. You can telephone or, better still, write for details, enclosing a stamped self-addressed envelope for a reply.

Beckfoot Mill
Prince Street
Dudley Hill
Bradford BD4 6HQ
Tel (0274) 651065

For Care Bears and other fur fabrics, polyester toy-filling; felt, and many other toy-making and craft materials.

Griffin Fabrics Ltd
The Craft Centre
97 Claremont Street
Aberdeen AB1 6QR
Tel (0224) 580798

For Care Bears and other fur fabrics, toy-filling, Binca embroidery fabric, glues, felt, wooden beads, seed beads, musical movements, lavender and pot-pourri, and many other toy-making and craft materials.

The Handicraft Shop
Northgate
Canterbury
Kent CT1 1BE
Tel (0227) 451188

For Care Bears and other fur fabrics, toy-filling, felt, dolls' house brick paper, dolly pegs, wooden beads, plastic granules for bean-bags, and many other toy-making and craft materials.

W Hobby Ltd
Knight's Hill Square
London SE27 0HH
Tel (01) 761 4244

For musical movements, dolls' house brick paper, doll's house plans and accessories, and many other craft materials and accessories.

USA

All materials used in this book will be readily available from your local supplier, but if necessary, the following mail order sources can supply fur fabrics, music boxes, etc:

The Crafty Teddy Inc
168 Seventh Street
Brooklyn
New York 11215

Merrily Doll Supply Co
8542 Ranchito Avenue
Panorama City
California 91402

INDEX